Name: _____

# I Have Good News For You

by Rev. Donald F. Ginkel

330,000 COPIES SOLD IN U.S. —
MORE THAN ONE-HALF MILLION WORLD WIDE

---

The love of God is greater far Than tongue or pen can ever tell;
It goes beyond the highest star, And reaches to the lowest hell;
The guilty pair, bowed down with care, God gave His Son to win;
His erring child He reconciled, And pardoned from his sin.
O love of God, how rich and pure! How measureless and strong!
It shall for evermore endure The saints' and angels' song.

— F. M. Lehman

---

Additional copies of this book plus other Bible studies for children and adults, confirmation, stewardship and evangelism materials may be ordered from the address below. Ask for a brochure.

**CHURCH PRESS, INC.**
Rev. Donald F. Ginkel
Toll Free Phone & Fax;
1-888-772-8878
www.churchpress.com

# A Word of Introduction

On a dark night on a road from Jackson to Vicksburg, MS, heavy rains washed a bridge away. When a truck driver saw the tail lights of the car ahead of him disappear, he knew something was wrong. Suddenly his own truck sailed silently through the black void where a bridge once stood, and he crashed into the river below. He made it out of the cab, swam to shore, and sat there in the darkness. Car after car zoomed into the gap and crashed into the swirling water below. Sixteen people died that night. Each of them had faith in a bridge that was no longer there.

Spiritually, there are millions of people today who have faith in a bridge that isn't there. So many people believe that by their good works, their character, their church membership, their morality, they will somehow cross the river of death to heaven. But the bridge is out! From Genesis to Revelation the message is the same. It is that God's Son, Jesus, has come, and He is the sure and only Bridge to heaven.

The bottom line of Christianity is that Jesus Christ satisfies in life and in death! People cannot give the satisfaction that man desires. Human nature says that a lot of friends, a lot of companionship, a lot of fellowship satisfies. But every friend will let you down. Every fellowship finally breaks up. Then you are alone — with your thoughts, your feelings, your desires.

The famous words of St. Augustine are still true today: "God, Thou hast made us for Thyself, and our hearts are restless until they rest in Thee."

You have at least three needs.

### Need No. 1: You Need To Know Who You Are

‖ A woman said, "I don't know who I am. I don't know why I am here. And I don't know where I am going." You know the feeling. Jesus came from the Father into this world to tell you that His Father made you and that the Son redeemed you on the cross so that you might have new life. He comes to give you worth, self-esteem, joy, peace, forgiveness, and a place in the family of God!

## Need No. 2: You Need To Know That You Are Loved

Someone said, "Just put your arm around me once in a while when I get mean." We all get mean. The Good News is that God is so powerful and His love so unlimited that He can hug you no matter how mean or hurting you may be. He loves you perfectly. He loves you totally. And He wants you to study the Bible from cover to cover to discover just how great His love is for you!

## Need No. 3: You Need Heaven

You are not going to be here very long. The Bible teaches that your life is like a flower and the grass, here today and cut down tomorrow. The Good News is that you are not going to disappear. You are going to live with God in eternity, on a new earth and in a mansion that He is already preparing for you. You possess this and own this now by your personal faith in Jesus. He promises, "I tell you the truth, he who believes has everlasting life" (John 6:47).

There are two basic objectives for this exciting course: 1. To learn about your needs and the solutions, especially, to learn to truly trust Jesus Christ as your personal Savior from sin and to receive that new and abundant life which comes only from Him. 2. To prepare you for meaningful membership in the Lutheran Church if you are not a member, and if you are, to better equip you for full-time service to Christ, to others, and to self.

We claim to be a Bible-centered, Bible-believing, and Bible-confessing Church. Our chief aim is to bring people to Christ. The critical question before you is: What am I going to do with Christ? Why did He die on the cross? How do I believe in Him as my Savior? What do I do after I come to faith?

We encourage you to participate fully in the lessons. React honestly and candidly. Be open to God's message to you. Ask questions. Is this really what God says? What does this Church believe? And listen. Listen carefully. God has some incredibly Good News for you.

Carefully complete the worksheets at the end of the lessons. Review your answers at the beginning of the next class. Faithfully follow the daily Bible reading schedule. Set aside a little quiet time each day for this. ● indicates a Bible verse for suggested memorization.

May God the Father, Son, and Holy Spirit instruct and direct you in your study.

**Soli Deo Gloria!**

*Contents*

# I Have Good News For You

## WELCOME

Scripture taken from the HOLY BIBLE: NEW INTERNATIONAL VERSION. Copyright 1978 by the International Bible Society. Used by permission of Zondervan Bible Publishers. Picture on page 43 Copyright © and used by permission of Concordia Publishing House. *I Have Good News For You* is available in braille. Write to Lutheran Library for the Blind, 3558 S. Jefferson Ave., St. Louis, MO 63118. Large print edition for visually impaired available from Church Press, Inc. Audio and video tapes are also available.

*I Have Good News For You*
Copyrighted © by Donald F. Ginkel, 1969
Revised edition copyrighted, 2001
All rights reserved

Library of Congress Catalog Card Number: A 107725

ISBN 0-9642122-2-6

Printed in the United States of America

I heard the voice of Jesus say,
"Come unto Me and rest;
Lay down, O weary one, lay down
Your head upon My breast."
I came to Jesus as I was,
So weary, worn, and sad;
I found in Him a resting-place,
And He has made me glad.

I heard the voice of Jesus say,
"Behold, I freely give
The living water, thirsty one,
Stoop down and drink and live."
I came to Jesus. And I drank
Of that life-giving stream;
My thirst was quenched, my soul revived,
And now I live in Him.

— Horatius Bonar

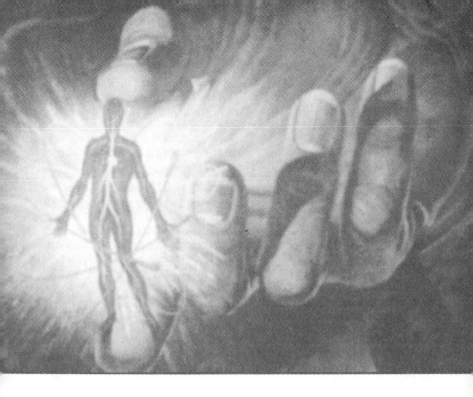

*Lesson 1*

## I HAVE GOOD NEWS FOR YOU

# About A God Who Cares For You

### 1. How can we know that there is a God?

PSALM 19:1  The *heavens declare* the glory of God; the *skies proclaim* the work of His hands.

ROMANS 1:19-20  What may be known about God is *plain to them,* because God has made it plain to them. For since the creation of the world God's *invisible qualities* — His eternal power and divine nature — *have been clearly seen,* being *understood from what has been made,* so that men are *without excuse.*

ROMANS 2:15  Gentiles show that the *requirements of the law are written on their hearts,* their *consciences* also *bearing witness,* and their thoughts now *accusing,* now even *defending* them.

To emphasize their belief that God played no role in the birth of their daughter, George and Tina Rollason, of York, PA, named her Atheistic Evolution Rollason. Mr. Rollason said that his daughter's name is the couple's response to other parents' use of Biblical names. "It's kind of cute once you say it a couple of times," said Mrs. Rollason. How pathetic! The little girl may some day shed many tears over her name. And what about God? "The One enthroned in heaven *laughs;* the Lord scoffs at them" (Psalm 2:4).

PSALM 14:1 The *fool* says in his heart, "*There is no God.*" They are corrupt, their deeds are vile; there is no one who does good.

Nature is dynamic proof that there is a God. The conscience, placed in every human by God, also declares that God exists. We call this the natural knowledge of God; it is there for all. The American Indians, the ancient Egyptians, and heathen throughout the world down through time have been convinced in the reality of God. Only fools (atheists and agnostics) deny the overwhelming evidence.

## 2. Who is the one true God?

MATTHEW 3:16-17 As soon as *Jesus* was baptized, He went up out of the water. At that moment heaven was opened, and He saw the *Spirit of God* descending like a dove and lighting on Him. And a *voice* from heaven said, "This is My Son, whom I love; with Him I am well pleased."

MATTHEW 28:19 Therefore go and make disciples of all nations, baptizing them in the name of the *Father* and of the *Son* and of the *Holy Spirit.*

DEUTERONOMY 6:4 Hear, O Israel: The LORD our God, the LORD is *one.*

There is only one true God but there are three distinct and

separate Persons [Triune, meaning three ("tri") in one ("unus")]. The Father made us, the Son redeemed us, and the Holy Spirit brings us to saving faith in Christ (The two well known creeds are the Apostles' Creed and the Nicene Creed which are carried on pages 118 to 120).

## 3. What is God like?

JOHN 4:24  God is *spirit,* and His worshipers must worship in spirit and in truth.

JOHN 1:18  No one has ever *seen* God.

PSALM 90:1-2  Lord, You have been our dwelling place throughout all generations. *Before* the mountains were born or You brought forth the earth and the world, *from everlasting to everlasting* You are God.

MALACHI 3:6  I the LORD *do not change.*

MATTHEW 19:26  With God *all things are possible.*

JEREMIAH 23:24  "Can anyone hide in *secret places* so that *I cannot see him?"* declares the LORD. "Do not *I fill heaven and earth?"* declares the LORD.

PSALM 139:1-4  O LORD, You have *searched me* and You *know me. You know* when I sit and when I rise; *You perceive my thoughts* from afar. *You discern* my going out and my lying down; *You are familiar* with all my ways. Before a word is on my tongue *You know it completely,* O LORD.

ISAIAH 6:3  *Holy, holy, holy* is the LORD Almighty.

DEUTERONOMY 32:4  He is the *Rock,* His works are *perfect,* and all His ways are *just.*

EXODUS 34:6-7   The LORD, the LORD, the *compassionate* and *gracious* God, slow to anger, *abounding* in *love* and *faithfulness, maintaining love* to thousands, and *forgiving* wickedness, rebellion and sin.

1 JOHN 4:8   God is *love.*

ISAIAH 46:8-9   *Remember* this, fix it in mind, take it to heart... *I am God,* and there is *none like Me.*

God is a **SPIRIT**. We **CANNOT SEE** Him. He is **FOREVER** and the **SAME** forever. This is wonderful for us. He is **ALL-POWERFUL**. He can do anything. God is **PRESENT EVERYWHERE** — a warning to unbelievers and a comfort to believers. He **KNOWS ALL** things. He knows everything about me. God is **HOLY**, absolutely pure and without sin. He cannot accept sin. We can come to God only because Jesus takes our sin away and makes us holy. God is **PERFECT** and **RIGHT**. God is **COMPASSIONATE**, **GRACIOUS**, and **FORGIVING**. He has patience with those who sin against Him. He shows mercy by forgiving all who ask for it through Jesus. God is **LOVE**. He loved every human being so much that He gave His only Son to be their Savior. His love for you is higher than the sky, deeper than the sea, and will last forever. There is **NO ONE LIKE HIM**. What a great God for us to love!

## 4. How did God make everything?

GENESIS 1:1   In the *beginning* God *created* the heavens and the earth.

GENESIS 1:3   And God said, *"Let there be... and there was..."*

EXODUS 20:11   In *six days* the LORD *made* the heavens and the earth, the sea, and *all* that is in them.

COLOSSIANS 1:16   By Him *all things* were created: things in *heaven* and on *earth, visible* and *invisible...* all things were created by Him and for Him.

GENESIS 2:7   The LORD *God formed the man from the dust* of the ground and *breathed into his nostrils the breath of life*, and the man became a living being.

GENESIS 1:26-27   Then God said, "Let us make man *in our image, in our likeness*, and *let them rule* over the fish of the sea and the birds of the air, over the livestock, over all the earth, and over all the creatures that move along the ground." So God created man in *His own image*, in the image of God He created him; male and female He created them.

GENESIS 1:31   God saw *all* that He had made, and it was *very good.*

God created the world out of nothing by His almighty Word over a period of six natural, consecutive days. This is the *creationist* view. (Two other opinions: *Atheistic evolution* says everything came about without help from a supernatural being, and *theistic evolution* says that a supernatural being aided the process of evolution.) God made everything perfect, including the angels in heaven. The crown of His creation was man. God made people like Himself — holy. He blessed them and gave them full authority to rule the earth.

## 5.  How did man fall away from God?

GENESIS 2:16-17   And the LORD God commanded the man, "You are *free to eat* from any tree in the garden; but you *must not eat* from the *tree of the knowledge of good and evil*, for when you eat of it *you will surely die.*"

GENESIS 3:1-7,9-10   Now the serpent was *more crafty* than any of the wild animals the LORD God had made. He said to the woman, "*Did God really say,* `You must not eat from any tree in the garden'?" The woman said to the serpent, "We may eat fruit from the trees in

the garden, but *God did say*, `You must not eat fruit from the tree that is in the middle of the garden, and you must not touch it, or you will die.'" "*You will not surely die*," the serpent said to the woman. "For God knows that when you eat of it *your eyes will be opened*, and *you will be like God*, knowing good *and evil.*" When the woman saw that the fruit of the tree was *good for food and pleasing to the eye*, and also *desirable for gaining wisdom*, *she* took some and *ate* it. She also gave some to her husband, who was with her, and *he ate* it. Then the *eyes* of both of them *were opened*, and they *realized they were naked*; so they sewed fig leaves together and made *coverings for themselves*. The LORD God called to the man, "Where are you?" He answered, "I heard You in the garden, and *I was afraid* because *I was naked; so I hid.*"

Adam and Eve had the choice of obeying God or disobeying (free will). God commanded them not to eat from the tree of the knowledge of good and evil. God wanted to see if they loved Him. But they disobeyed God, and they plunged the human race into sin. This is called original sin (Romans 5:12; Psalm 51:5). Sin is rebellion against a loving God and brings sad results: a guilty conscience, a spiritual void, and death as God promised. (For information on evil angels read 2 Peter 2:4 and Jude 6.)

## 6. How did God plan to win man back again?

GENESIS 3:15 I will put *enmity* between you and the woman, and between your offspring (or seed) and hers; *He will crush* your head, and *you will strike* His heel.

● JOHN 3:16 For God *so loved* the world that He gave His one and only Son, that whoever *believes* in Him shall *not perish* but *have eternal life.*

God provided a way for mankind to escape the penalty for sin. He promised man a Savior, the woman's Seed, who would pay the penalty for man's sins and crush Satan. Through His sacrifice on the cross Christ saved all people from Satan's tyranny. We know that God loves us. He sent Jesus to suffer and die for us. When we truly believe in Jesus, we will not die but will live with Him forever. This is God's promise to us.

## 7. How does God care for us today?

JOB 33:4 The Spirit of God *has made me*, the breath of the *Almighty gives me life.*

MATTHEW 10:29-31 Are not two sparrows sold for a penny? Yet not one of them will fall to the ground apart from the will of your Father. And even the *very hairs of your head are all numbered.* So *don't be afraid;* you are *worth more* than many sparrows.

1 JOHN 3:1-2 How great is the *love the Father has lavished on us,* that we should be called *children of God!* And that is what we are! The reason the world does not know us is that it did not know Him. Dear friends, *now we are children of God.*

God demonstrates His great love for us today, too. He made us and gives us life. He cares for us daily and gives us only those things which will bless us. His greatest act of love is this — He forgives us all our sins for Jesus' sake, calls us His very own, and will continue to do this in the future.

## 8. What can we give God for all His love?

GENESIS 32:10 *I am unworthy* of all the kindness and faithfulness You have shown Your servant.

PSALM 118:1 *Give thanks to the LORD,* for He is good; His love endures forever.

1 CORINTHIANS 10:31 So whether you eat or drink or whatever you do, *do it all for the glory of God.*

GALATIANS 6:10 Therefore, as we have opportunity, let us *do good to all people, especially* to those who belong to *the family of believers.*

MARK 16:15-16 Jesus said to them, "*Go* into all the world and *preach the good news* to all creation. Whoever believes and is baptized will be saved, but whoever does not believe will be condemned."

We do not deserve to get any of God's blessings. And so we thank God. We live, work, and play to the glory of His name. We tell other people the Good News that God loves them, too. Then, those people can live with Him forever also.

## 9. What does it mean to believe in God?

JAMES 2:19 You *believe* that there is one God. Good! Even *the demons believe* that — and shudder.

JOHN 17:3 Now this is eternal life: that they may *know You*, the only *true God*, and *Jesus Christ*, whom You have sent.

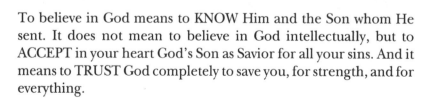

● JOHN 3:36 Whoever *believes in the Son has eternal life*, but whoever rejects the Son will not see life, for God's wrath remains on him.

ISAIAH 12:2 Surely *God is my salvation*; I will *trust* and not be afraid. The LORD, the LORD, is my strength and my song; He has become my salvation.

To believe in God means to KNOW Him and the Son whom He sent. It does not mean to believe in God intellectually, but to ACCEPT in your heart God's Son as Savior for all your sins. And it means to TRUST God completely to save you, for strength, and for everything.

## Let's pray together

Almighty and Triune God, Father, Son, and Holy Spirit, we thank You for letting us study these Scripture verses together. You have told us that You are a caring and loving God. If we did not know You we would be worshiping some false god. Thank You for all You've done. You've poured out a thousand blessings upon us. Thank You for sending Jesus to save us from our sins. We are so happy to know that You are eager to forgive us. Thank You for our food, clothing, and shelter. Thank You for this Bible study. Help us tell our friends all about You. Bless us as we study the Bible at home. Bring us all safely together again a week from now. Assist us in bringing a friend along with us. Hear us for Jesus' sake. Amen.

## Let's sing together

O Lord my God! When I in awesome wonder
Consider all the worlds Thy hands have made.
I see the stars, I hear the rolling thunder,
Thy pow'r throughout the universe displayed.
*Refrain:*
Then sings my soul, my Savior God to Thee;
How great Thou art, how great Thou art!
Then sings my soul, my Savior God to Thee;
How great Thou art, how great Thou art!

And when I think that God, His Son not sparing,
Sent Him to die, I scarce can take it in;
That on the Cross, my burden gladly bearing,
He bled and died to take away my sin. *Refrain*

## Bible reading schedule for the next seven days

❑  1st day – John 1
❑  2nd day – John 2
❑  3rd day – John 3
❑  4th day – John 4

❑  5th day – John 5
❑  6th day – John 6
❑  7th day – John 7

## Worksheet no. 1

1.  From what two sources can all men know that there is a God?

_____ and _____

2. True or False: The true God is three Gods: Father, Son, and Holy Spirit.

3. True or False: The Father was first, then Jesus, then the Holy Spirit.

4. God is a _____ and no human eye has seen Him. God never had a _____ and will have no _____ . God is always the _____. All things are _____ _____ with God. He is present everywhere and no one can _____ from Him. God knows when I _____ down and _____ up. My life is an open _____ to Him. He is also holy which means He is _____ _____. He always keeps the _____ He makes. The greatest way in which He shows His mercy is when He _____ those who _____ against Him. God truly _____ me and sent His _____ to be my _____

5. a.  The Bible says God made the world. Evolution says _____
      _____

   b.  The Bible says God created all things in six days. Evolution says _____

   c.  The Bible says God made man and gave him a rational soul. Evolution says _____

6. Mention three ways in which God cares for you. List the best way last.

a. _____

b. _____

c. _____

7. What is sin? _____

8. Write the Bible reference containing the first promise of a Savior. _____

9. How did God plan to win men back to Himself? _____

_____

10. True or False: God cares for us because He feels sorry for us.

11. True or False: The way to be saved is to believe in God.

12. What can you give God for all His love for you? _____

_____

*Lesson 2*

## I HAVE GOOD NEWS FOR YOU

# About A Bible Which Guides and Frees You

### 1. What is the Bible?

1 PETER 1:10 Concerning this salvation, the *prophets*, who *spoke of the grace that was to come* to you, searched intently and with the greatest care.

2 PETER 1:21 For prophecy never had its origin in the will of man, but *men spoke* from God *as they were carried along by the Holy Spirit.*

2 TIMOTHY 3:16 *All Scripture* is *God-breathed.*

JOHN 17:17 Sanctify them by the truth; Your *word is truth.*

PSALM 119:105 Your word is a *lamp* to my feet and a *light* for my path.

JOHN 20:30-31 Jesus did *many other miraculous signs* in the presence of His disciples, which are not recorded in this book. But *these are written that you may believe* that Jesus is the Christ, the Son of God, and that *by believing you may have life in His name.*

REVELATION 22:18-19 I warn everyone who hears the words of the prophecy of this book: If anyone *adds anything* to them, God will add to him the plagues described in this book. And if anyone *takes words away* from this book of prophecy, God will take away from him his share in the tree of life and in the holy city, which are described in this book.

The Greek words for "the Bible" mean "the Book"; it's above all others. Testament means will or agreement. Men called prophets wrote the 39 books of the Old Testament in Hebrew at the direction of the Holy Spirit. Their message centered on God's grace, the promise of a Messiah. The 27 books of the New Testament were written in Greek by the apostles and evangelists after Christ's death. All of the Bible is inspired or "God-breathed." It is wholly true. It is like a brilliant light to light up the path that leads to heaven. Not everything Jesus did is in the Bible, but what is there is there so you may have life in His name. God warns people not to add anything to or take anything away from it.

## 2. What are the two great messages of the Bible?

LEVITICUS 19:2 *Be holy* because I, the LORD your God, am holy.

EXODUS 20:3ff You *shall...* You *shall not...*

1 JOHN 4:9 This is how *God showed His love* among us: *He sent His one and only Son* into

the world that we might *live* through Him.

JOHN 3:16  For *God so loved the world* that *He gave His one and only Son,* that whoever *believes in Him* shall not perish but *have eternal life.*

ROMANS 1:16  I am not ashamed of the Gospel, because it is the *power of God for the salvation* of everyone who believes.

The Law and Gospel are the two great messages of the Bible. The Law is the holy will of God in which He tells us how to be, holy, and what we are to do and not to do. In the Law the activity is on the part of man. In the Gospel the activity is on the part of God. It is the Good News that Jesus is our Savior. The Law shows us our sins, condemns us, and pronounces death. The Gospel shows us a Savior and gives us life.

## 3.  How does the Law guide us?

### First Commandment

EXODUS 20:3  **You shall have no other gods before Me.**

MATTHEW 22:37-38  Jesus replied: "'*Love the Lord* your God with *all your heart* and with *all your soul* and with *all your mind.*' This is the first and greatest commandment."

ISAIAH 42:8  *I am the LORD;* that is My name! I will not give *My glory to another* or *My praise to idols.*

JOHN 5:22-23  The Father has entrusted all judgment to the Son, *that all may honor the Son just as they honor the Father.* He who *does not honor the Son does not honor the Father,* who sent Him.

EPHESIANS 5:5  For of this you can be sure: *No immoral, impure or greedy* person — *such a man is an idolater* — has any inheritance in the Kingdom of Christ and of God.

PSALM 33:8  Let all the earth *fear the LORD;* let all the people of the world *revere Him.*

PROVERBS 23:26  My son, *give Me your heart* and let your eyes *keep to My ways.*

This is the foremost commandment. God forbids worship of any idols, money, job, home, family, saints or statues. God insists that He occupy first place in our lives and that we make a full commitment to Him. We are to love, trust, and believe in Him more than anyone or anything else.

## Second Commandment

EXODUS 20:7  **You shall not misuse the name of the LORD your God.**

EXODUS 20:7  The Lord will not hold anyone *guiltless* who *misuses His name.*

JAMES 3:9-10  With the tongue *we praise our Lord* and Father, and with it *we curse men,* who have been made in God's likeness. Out of the same mouth come *praise and cursing.* My brothers, this should not be.

LEVITICUS 19:12  *Do not swear falsely* by My name and so *profane* the name of your God.

LEVITICUS 19:31  Do not turn to *mediums* or seek out *spiritists,* for you will be *defiled* by them. I am the LORD your God.

PSALM 50:15  *Call upon Me* in the day of trouble; I will deliver you, and *you will honor Me.*

PSALM 103:1  *Praise the LORD,* O my soul; *all my inmost being,* praise His holy name.

God's name is holy. He forbids using it carelessly. Cursing is asking for God's wrath on some person or object. Swearing is using His name to assert truthfulness to something you said or did. Thoughtless expressions such as "oh, my god," "good heavens," "by gosh," etc., are also sinful. Witchcraft, lying, or deceiving by His name are forbidden. We should believe, confess, and spread His name and call on Him in prayer and praise.

## Third Commandment

EXODUS 20:8 **Remember the Sabbath day by keeping it holy**.

COLOSSIANS 2:16-17 *Do not let anyone judge* you by what you eat or drink, or with regard to a religious festival, a New Moon celebration or a Sabbath day. *These are a shadow* of the *things* that were *to come; the reality,* however, *is* found in *Christ.*

ACTS 2:42 They (the 3,000 new believers) *devoted* themselves to the *apostles' teaching* and to the *fellowship,* to the *breaking of bread* and to *prayer.*

JOHN 8:47 He who *belongs* to God *hears* what God says. The reason you *do not hear* is that you *do not belong* to God.

LUKE 11:28 Jesus replied, "*Blessed* rather are those who *hear* the word of God and *obey* it."

HEBREWS 13:17 *Obey* your leaders and *submit* to their authority. They keep watch over you as men who must give an account. Obey them so that *their work will be a joy, not a burden,* for that would be of no advantage to you.

The early Christians chose Sunday as their special day of worship because Jesus rose from the dead on this day and because God began the creation of the world on Sunday. We break this commandment by not coming to church at all, by coming irregularly, by not listening, by not believing, or not doing what the Word tells us to do. God promises a special joy to all who study and obey His Word and to those who obey and follow their spiritual leader, their pastor.

## Fourth Commandment

EXODUS 20:12  **Honor your father and your mother, so that you may live long in the land the LORD your God is giving you.**

EPHESIANS 6:1-4  Children, *obey your parents* in the Lord, for *this is right.* "*Honor your father and mother*" — which is the first commandment with a promise — "that it may go well with you and that you may enjoy long life on the earth." Fathers, *do not exasperate* your children; instead, bring them up in the *training and instruction of the Lord.*

ROMANS 13:1-2  Everyone must *submit himself to the governing authorities,* for there is no authority except that which God has established. The authorities that exist have been established by God. Consequently, *he who rebels against the authority is rebelling against what God has instituted,* and those who do so will bring judgment on themselves.

1 PETER 2:18-19  Slaves, *submit yourselves to your masters* with all respect, not only to those who are good and considerate, but also to those who are harsh. For it is commendable if a man *bears up under the pain of unjust suffering because he is conscious of God.*

ACTS 5:29  We *must obey God* rather than men!

God puts people over us in the home, school, state, and church. We are to honor them by obeying, serving, and loving them. This is pleasing to God. This is the only commandment with a special promise of blessing such as long life.

## Fifth Commandment

EXODUS 20:13  **You shall not murder**

GENESIS 9:6  Whoever sheds the blood of man, *by man shall his blood be shed;* for in the image of God has God made man.

ROMANS 13:4  He (the government) is *God's servant* to do you good.

But if you do wrong, be afraid, for he does not bear the sword for nothing. *He is God's servant*, an agent of wrath *to bring punishment on the wrongdoer.*

ROMANS 12:19 *Do not take revenge*, my friends, but *leave room for God's wrath*, for it is written: "*It is Mine to avenge; I will repay*," says the Lord.

1 JOHN 3:15 Anyone who *hates his brother is a murderer*, and you know that no murderer has eternal life in him.

EPHESIANS 4:32 Be *kind* and *compassionate* to one another, *forgiving* each other, just as in Christ God forgave you.

God is the giver of life and reserves the right to take it. A person's most valuable earthly possession is his life. God forbids us to hurt our neighbor in any way — physically or emotionally. We should never take revenge. We should take care of our minds and bodies and do the same for others.

## Sixth Commandment

EXODUS 20:14 **You shall not commit adultery**.

MATTHEW 19:6 So they are no longer *two*, but *one*. Therefore what *God has joined* together, *let man not separate.*

"For this reason a man will leave his father & mother and be united to his wife, and the two will become **one flesh**". Ephesians 5:31

MATTHEW 19:9 I tell you that anyone who *divorces his wife*, except for marital unfaithfulness, and marries another woman *commits adultery*.

1 CORINTHIANS 7:15 If the *unbeliever leaves*, let him do so. A *believing* man or woman *is not bound* in such circumstances.

EPHESIANS 5:24-25 As the *church submits* to Christ, so also *wives* should *submit to their husbands* in everything. *Husbands, love* your *wives,* just *as Christ loved the church* and gave Himself up for her.

MATTHEW 15:19  *Out of the heart come* evil thoughts, murder, adultery, sexual immorality, theft, false testimony, slander.

MATTHEW 5:28  I tell you that *anyone who looks at a woman lustfully* has *already committed adultery with her in his heart.*

1 CORINTHIANS 6:18-20  He who *sins sexually sins against his own body.* Do you not know that your *body is a temple* of the Holy Spirit, who is in you, whom you have received from God? You are not your own; you were bought at a price. Therefore *honor God with your body.*

Marriage is an ordinance of God for the happiness, procreation, and morality of the human family. Marriage is for life and is entered into by engagement. Adultery and malicious desertion are the only Biblical grounds for divorce. God wants our lives and actions to be pure. Bible study, prayer, hard work and play, avoiding certain people and places help us stay pure.

## Seventh Commandment

EXODUS 20:15  **You shall not steal.**

LEVITICUS 19:35  Do not use *dishonest standards* when measuring *length, weight* or *quantity.*

JEREMIAH 22:13  Woe to him (King Jehoiachin) who builds his palace *by unrighteousness,* his upper rooms *by injustice,* making his countrymen *work for nothing,* not paying them for their labor.

2 THESSALONIANS 3:10  If a man *will not work,* he *shall not eat.*

1 PETER 4:10  Each one should use whatever *gift he has received to serve others,* faithfully administering *God's grace* in its various forms.

Owning property is a God-given right; to some He gives more and to others less. But man does not really own — God owns and man owes. Man is a steward (manager) of God's possessions loaned to him. Employers are to pay their employees good salaries. Employees are to do their best work in return. We should use our possessions for our own, our neighbor's, and God's good.

## Eighth Commandment

EXODUS 20:16  **You shall not give false testimony against your neighbor.**

PROVERBS 19:5  A *false witness* will not go unpunished, and he who pours out *lies* will not go free.

PROVERBS 11:13  A *gossip betrays a confidence*, but a *trustworthy* man *keeps a secret*.

ZECHARIAH 8:17 "*Do not plot evil* against your neighbor, and do not love to *swear falsely*. I hate all this," declares the LORD.

PROVERBS 31:8-9  *Speak up for those who cannot speak* for themselves, for the rights of all who are destitute. *Speak up* and *judge fairly; defend the rights* of the poor and needy.

A person's name and reputation are very important. That can quickly be destroyed by lies and gossip. Once hurtful words are spoken, they cannot be retracted. Three tests for speaking about someone might be: 1. Is it true? 2. Is it needful? 3. Is it kind?

## Ninth and Tenth Commandments

EXODUS 20:17  **You shall not covet your neighbor's house. You shall not covet your neighbor's wife, or his manservant or maidservant, his ox or donkey, or anything that belongs to your neighbor.**

JAMES 4:2 You *want something* but don't get it. You *kill and covet*, but you cannot have *what you want*. You *quarrel and fight*. You do not have, because *you do not ask God.*

PSALM 37:4  *Delight yourself in the LORD and He will give you the desires of your heart.*

It is not wrong to want to get ahead, but it is sin to wish to have something at someone else's expense. Covetousness is the base desire for what one has not and which has its basis in discontentment with what one has.

## 4. How does the Law condemn us?

● MATTHEW 5:48  *Be perfect,* therefore, *as* your heavenly Father is perfect.

JAMES 2:10  For whoever keeps the whole law and yet *stumbles at just one point* is *guilty of breaking all of it.*

● PSALM 14:3  *All have turned aside,* they have *together become corrupt;* there is *no one who does good,* not even one.

ROMANS 3:20  No one will be *declared righteous* in His sight by *observing the law,* rather, through the law we become *conscious of sin.*

● ROMANS 6:23  For the *wages of sin* is *death.*

How many of God's laws must we obey to get into heaven? Not 65%, not 99%, but 100% — perfection! We have failed the entrance exam! Only a brief look at the commandments quickly shows that we have broken each of them (this is actual sin in contrast to original sin which we inherit). Beside sins of commission, we also sin when we should have done something and did nothing (sins of omission). As the bathroom mirror reveals how we look when rising early in the morning, so the perfect mirror of God's Law shows us as we are spiritually, sinners, with the sentence of physical and eternal death upon us.

## 5. How does the Gospel free us?

ROMANS 10:4 Christ is the *end of the law* so that there may be *righteousness* for every one who *believes.*

GALATIANS 3:13 Christ *redeemed us from the curse* of the law by becoming a curse for us.

GALATIANS 3:21-22 Is the law, therefore, opposed to the promises of God? Absolutely not! For if a law had been given that could impart life, then righteousness would certainly have come by the law. But the Scripture declares that the whole world is a prisoner of sin, so that *what was promised,* being *given* through *faith* in Jesus Christ, might be *given* to those who *believe.*

The Good News is that Jesus took our place under the curse of the Law and has freed us from our sins and from eternal death. He paid the penalty for our sins. He kept all the demands of the Law which were upon us. Now we are free, forgiven, and redeemed. You may receive this GIFT right now. Confess your sins to Him. Believe in Jesus in your heart right now, just as you are. Jesus will come into your heart and life and the promised gift WILL be your very own. This is His promise.

### Let's pray together

Lord God, our Father, we praise You for the gift of Your holy Word, the Bible! Surely it is the Book of books in which we find an honest description of our utter depravity, our inability to save ourselves, and the marvelous message of the sacrifice of Your only Son, Jesus Christ, on the Cross. Bless our study of the Book in this study group, in church, and in our homes. Help us to erect the family altar in our homes so that we may feed daily upon this satisfying bread of life and may live. For Jesus' sake hear our prayer, forgive us our sins and short-comings, help us to bring our friends to You, and lead us on a closer walk with You this week. Amen.

## Let's sing together

My faith looks up to Thee, Thou Lamb of Calvary, Savior divine!
Now hear me while I pray, Take all my guilt away,
O let me from this day Be wholly Thine!

May Thy rich grace impart Strength to my fainting heart, My zeal
inspire; As Thou hast died for me, O may my love to Thee
Pure, warm, and changeless be, A living fire!

When ends life's passing dream, When death's cold, threatening
stream Shall o'er me roll, Blest Savior, then, in love,
Fear and distrust remove; O lift me safe above, A ransomed soul!

## Bible reading schedule for the next seven days

- ❑  1$^{st}$ day – John 8
- ❑  2$^{nd}$ day – John 9
- ❑  3$^{rd}$ day – John 10
- ❑  4$^{th}$ day – John 11
- ❑  5$^{th}$ day – John 12
- ❑  6$^{th}$ day – John 13
- ❑  7$^{th}$ day – John 14

## Worksheet no. 2

1. The Bible (    ) contains the Word of God, (    ) is the Word
   of God and men, (    ) is the Word of God.

2. True or False: The main reason why the Bible was written is
   that it may show us how to live.

3. True or False: The main theme of the Bible is that God is kind,
   gentle, and good.

4. The _____ brings us to a knowledge of our sins. The

   _____ brings us to a knowledge of our Savior.

5. There are ____ books in the Old Testament and ____ books

   in the New Testament for a total of _____ books. The Old

Testament was written in the _____ language by men

called _____, and the New Testament was written in the

_____ language by men called _____

and _____ In the original the words, "The Bible,"

really mean _____. The word "testament"

means_____

6. True or False: We can prove to anyone that the Bible is true.

7. Name several religious groups which sin against the message

of John 5:23 and state why: _____

_____

8. The early Christians chose Sunday as their special day of worship because (   ) it was usually a sunny day, (   ) God commanded it, (   ) Christ rose from the dead on this day.

9. True or False: I have never committed adultery or murder.

10. "Mirror, mirror on the wall. Who is the fairest of them all?"

What does the mirror of God's Law tell you? _____

_____

11. True or False: God's Law says that all have sinned and that the wages of sin is death, physical and eternal.

12. What must you do to become a Christian? _____

_____

_____

13. True or False: Even after one becomes a Christian, he can and will sin.

14. What two messages should you share to bring a person to Christ? _____

_____

15. True or False: From the Gospel I know for certain that I am forgiven of all my sin. If I die tonight, I will go to heaven for sure.

*Lesson 3*

## I HAVE GOOD NEWS FOR YOU

# About A Savior Who Saves You

### 1. What are some important promises of a coming Savior?

MICAH 5:2 But you, *Bethlehem* Ephrathah, though you are small among the clans of Judah, out of you will come for Me One who will be *Ruler over Israel.*

ISAIAH 7:14 The *virgin* will be with Child and will give birth to a Son, and will call Him *Immanuel.*

ISAIAH 9:6 For to us a *Child* is born, to us a

*Son* is given, and the government will be on His shoulders. And He will be called *Wonderful Counselor, Mighty God, Everlasting Father, Prince of Peace.*

ISAIAH 53:5-6   But He *was pierced* for our transgressions, He *was crushed* for our iniquities; the *punishment* that brought us peace was upon Him, and by *His wounds* we are healed. We all, like sheep, have gone astray, each of us has turned to his own way; and the *LORD has laid on Him the iniquity of us all.*

From Genesis 3:15 on through the Old Testament the single, common thread is the infinite love of God for mankind in Christ. Over 300 Old Testament verses clearly promise that the Savior is coming and His task: the redemption of the whole human race from sin. Even the names given Him, such as Immanuel, meaning "God with us," show His mission and purpose.

## 2.   What is significant about Jesus' birth and early life?

LUKE 1:28,31,32,34,35,37   The angel went to Mary and said, "Greetings, you who are highly favored! The Lord is with you... *You will be with Child* and give birth to a Son, and you are to give Him the name *Jesus*. He will be great and will be called the Son of the Most High..." "*How will this be*," Mary asked the angel, "*since I am a virgin?*" The angel answered, "The *Holy Spirit will come upon you* and the power of the Most High will overshadow you. So the *holy One* to be born will be *called the Son of God...* For *nothing is impossible* with God."

MATTHEW 1:20-23   An angel of the Lord appeared to him in a dream and said, "Joseph son of David, do not be afraid to take Mary home as your wife, because what is conceived in her is *from the Holy Spirit.* She will give birth to a Son, and you are to give Him the name *Jesus,* because He will *save His people from their sins.*" All this took place to *fulfill what the Lord had said* through the prophet: "The *virgin* will be with Child and will give birth to a Son, and they will call Him *Immanuel*" — which means, "God with us."

LUKE 2:6,7,10-12,16,21,40,49,52 While they were in *Bethlehem,* the time came for the Baby to be born, and she gave birth to her firstborn, a Son. She wrapped Him in cloths and placed Him in a manger, because there was no room for them in the inn... The angel said to the shepherds, "Do not be afraid. I bring you *good news of great joy* that will be *for all the people.* Today in the *town of David* a Savior has been born to you; He is *Christ the Lord.* This will be a *sign* to you: You will find a Baby *wrapped in cloths* and *lying in a manger*"... So *they hurried off* and *found* Mary and Joseph, and *the Baby*, who was lying in the manger... On the eighth day, when it was time to circumcise Him, *He was named Jesus*... And the Child *grew* and became *strong*; He was *filled with wisdom*, and the *grace of God was upon Him*... "Why were you searching for Me?" He asked. "Didn't you know I had to be in My Father's house?"... And Jesus *grew* in *wisdom* and *stature*, and in *favor with God* and *men.*

MATTHEW 2:13-15  An angel of the Lord appeared to Joseph in a dream. "Get up," he said, "take the Child and His mother and escape to Egypt. Stay there until I tell you, for Herod is going to *search for the Child to kill Him.*" So he got up, took the Child and His mother during the night and left for Egypt, where he stayed until the death of Herod. And so was *fulfilled what the Lord had said through the prophet:* "Out of Egypt I called My Son."

By a miracle of the Holy Spirit the eternal Son of God received a body in the virgin Mary. His name, Jesus, means "Savior." Christ means "the Anointed One." He was anointed to be our Prophet (Teacher — Matthew 17:5), our Priest (who would sacrifice Himself on the Cross — Hebrews 7:26-27), and our King (who would rule His Church and the world — Philippians 2:10-11). Everything about Jesus clearly points to His role as man's Savior from sin, Satan, and eternal death. Following His appearance in the Temple at age twelve nothing is said of our Lord until He is thirty. He goes to the Jordan river where John is preaching and baptizing. He is baptized, chooses twelve disciples, lives a life of poverty, travels and preaches constantly, performs innumerable miracles, and proves Himself to be God's Son and the Savior of the world. Some believe in Him, but many others reject Him, and his enemies plot His death.

### 3.  What two natures are united in Christ?

1 TIMOTHY 2:5-6  There is one God and one *Mediator between* God and men, the *man* Christ Jesus, who gave Himself as a ransom for all men.

MATTHEW 17:5  A voice from the cloud said, "*This is My Son,* whom I love; with Him I am well pleased. Listen to Him!"

1 JOHN 5:20  We know also that the *Son of God* has come... Jesus Christ. He is the *true God* and eternal life.

Christ was both God and Man. He had to be man so that He might take our place under the Law and that He might be able to suffer and die in our stead. He had to be true God so that He could keep the Law perfectly and that His suffering and death would be sufficient and complete.

### 4.  How did Christ suffer and die?

JOHN 10:18  No one takes My life from Me, but *I lay it down of My own accord.*

MATTHEW 26:38-39 Jesus said to them, "My *soul is overwhelmed with sorrow to the point of death.* Stay here and keep watch with Me." Going a little farther, He fell with His face to the ground and prayed, "My Father, if it is possible, *may this cup be taken from Me.* Yet not as I will, but as You will."

MATTHEW 27:28-30,33-35,39,44-46  They stripped Him and put a *scarlet robe* on Him, and then wove a *crown of thorns* and set it on His head. They put a *staff* in His right hand and *knelt* in front of Him and *mocked* Him. "Hail, King of the Jews!" they said. They *spit* on Him, and took the staff and *struck* Him on the head *again and again....* They came to a place called Golgotha (which means The

Place of the Skull). There they offered Him wine to drink, mixed with gall; but after tasting it, He *refused to drink it.* When they had *crucified* Him, they *divided up His clothes* by casting lots... Those who passed by *hurled insults* at Him, *shaking their heads...* In the same way the robbers who were crucified with Him also *heaped insults* on Him. From the sixth hour until the ninth hour *darkness* came over all the land. About the ninth hour Jesus cried out in a loud voice,

"Eloi, Eloi, lama sabachthani?" — which means, *"My God, My God, why have You forsaken Me?"*

JOHN 19:28,30  Later, knowing that *all was now completed...* Jesus said, *"It is finished."* With that, He bowed His head and *gave up His spirit.*

MATTHEW 27:51,52,54,59,60,65,66  At that moment the curtain of the temple was *torn in two* from top to bottom. The *earth shook* and the *rocks split.* The *tombs broke open* and the *bodies* of many holy people who had died were *raised to life...* When the centurion and those with Him who were guarding Jesus saw the earthquake and all that had happened, they were terrified, and exclaimed, *"Surely He was the Son of God!"...* Joseph took the body, wrapped it in a *clean linen cloth,* and placed it in his own *new tomb* that he had cut out of the rock. He rolled a *big stone* in front of the entrance to the tomb... "Take a guard," Pilate answered. "Go, *make the tomb* as *secure* as you know how." So they went and made the tomb secure by putting a *seal* on the stone and *posting the guard.*

Of His own free will our Lord suffered unimaginable agony of body and soul. At 9:00 He was nailed to the cross. At 12:00 darkness covered the land. The Father completely forsook Jesus. Jesus experienced hell. Finally, at 3:00, He had endured the suffering for every sin and every sinner. He cried from the cross for the sixth time, "It is finished!" Hell, death, and the devil were conquered. We have all been redeemed. This is the Good News. It is the greatest news we can hear and believe.

## 5. What does the Bible say about Jesus' resurrection and ascension?

1 PETER 3:18-19 He was put to death in
the body but made alive by the Spirit,
through whom also *He went and preached
to the spirits in prison.*

MATTHEW 28:1-2,5-7,9 After the Sabbath, *at
dawn* on the first day of the week, Mary
Magdalene and the other Mary went to look at
the tomb. There was a *violent earthquake,* for an
angel of the Lord came down from heaven and,
going to the tomb, *rolled back the stone* and sat on it... The angel said
to the women, "Do not be afraid, for I know that you are looking
for Jesus, who was crucified. *He is not here; He has risen, just as He
said. Come and see* the place where He lay. Then *go quickly and tell*
His disciples: 'He has risen from the dead and is going ahead of
you into Galilee. There *you will see Him...*'" Suddenly Jesus met
them. "*Greetings,*" He said. They came to Him, clasped His feet and
*worshiped* Him.

ACTS 1:3 After His suffering, He showed himself to these men and
gave *many convincing proofs* that He was alive. He appeared to them
over a period of *forty days* and spoke about the Kingdom of God.

**Jesus' arrival in
Bethlehem was utterly
unique — so was His
departure near Bethany.**

LUKE 24:50-52 When He had led them
out to the vicinity of Bethany, He lifted
up His hands and *blessed* them. While
He was blessing them, *He left them and
was taken up into heaven.* Then they
*worshiped* Him and returned to Jerusalem with *great joy.*

ROMANS 8:34 Christ Jesus, who *died* — more than that, who was
*raised* to life — is at the right hand of God and is also *interceding for
us.*

Being made alive spiritually, Christ descended into hell, not to
suffer, but to proclaim His victory over Satan and his followers. No
power on earth could keep Him in the grave. When the women
came to the grave, they were greeted by a holy angel, an empty
tomb, and a message of joy. Soon Jesus showed Himself to the

women and the rest of the disciples and offered insurmountable proof of His resurrection. He instructed His disciples, commissioned them to make disciples of all people, promised the power of the Holy Spirit, and then ascended into heaven. Now we know God has accepted Jesus' sacrifice on our behalf as satisfactory for our redemption. We have been brought back to God, and because He lives and intercedes for us we, too, shall live with Him soon in unending glory.

## 6. What did Christ really accomplish?

GALATIANS 4:4-5 When the time had fully come, God sent His Son, born of a woman, born under Law, to *redeem those under Law,* that we might receive the *full rights of sons.*

● 1 JOHN 4:9 This is how God showed His love among us: He sent His one and only Son into the world that we might *live through Him.*

1 JOHN 3:8 He who does what is sinful is of the devil, because the devil has been sinning from the beginning. The reason the Son of God appeared was to *destroy the devil's work.*

JOHN 8:34,36 Jesus replied, "I tell you the truth, everyone who sins is a slave to sin... So if the Son *sets you free,* you will be *free indeed.*"

2 TIMOTHY 1:10 Christ Jesus has *destroyed death* and has *brought life* and *immortality to light* through the Gospel.

By His suffering, death, and resurrection Jesus not only defeated the devil, but conquered sin and hell and restored peace between God and man. When Christ Jesus frees a sinner from his enemies, he is really free, and he has fellowship in God's family. Lidie Edmunds wrote —

> *The great Physician heals the sick, The lost He came to save;*
> *For me His precious blood He shed, For me His life He gave.*
> *I need no other evidence, I need no other plea;*
> *It is enough that Jesus died And rose again for me.*

## 7. Who receives these wonderful blessings?

● LUKE 19:10 The Son of Man came to seek and to *save what was lost.*

1 JOHN 2:2 Jesus Christ is the *atoning sacrifice* for our sins, and not only for ours but also for the *sins of the whole world.*

2 PETER 2:1 They *deny* the sovereign Lord who bought them — *bringing swift destruction on themselves.*

JOHN 3:16 For God so loved the *world* that He gave His one and only Son, that *whoever believes in Him* shall not perish but *have eternal life.*

The benefits of salvation are for everyone. All have been redeemed. All sins are forgiven. Only those who deny their Lord deny also these blessings and receive in their place destruction. God's love, however, goes out to all. He invites everyone to come. He promises that whoever believes in Jesus has, in place of death, everlasting life. What Good News this is — to believe and to share!

### Let's pray together

Lord Jesus, we thank You for all You have done to be our Savior. When we see You on the cross, we realize what a terrible thing sin is. People beat You, crowned You with thorns, spit on You, and killed you — for us. Forgive us for having made Your cross so heavy by our sins. Because You came out of the grave alive we know that we, too, shall be raised from the dead on the last day. Strengthen our faith. Help us love and trust You more. Help us share this Good News with others. We dedicate ourselves to You, dear Lord. We praise You and love You. Amen.

### Let's sing together

When I survey the wondrous cross
On which the Prince of glory died,
My richest gain I count but loss
And pour contempt on all my pride.

See, from His head, His hands, His feet,
Sorrow and love flow mingled down,
Did e'er such love and sorrow meet
Or thorns compose so rich a crown.

Were the whole realm of nature mine,
That were a tribute far too small;
Love so amazing, so divine,
Demands my soul, my life, my all!

**Bible reading schedule for the next seven days**

- ❑  1st day – John 15
- ❑  2nd day – John 16
- ❑  3rd day – John 17
- ❑  4th day – John 18

- ❑  5th day – John 19
- ❑  6th day – John 20
- ❑  7th day – John 21

**Worksheet no. 3**

1. (    ) Most, (    ) Many, (    ) Few of the Old Testament people could understand the Messianic prophecies.

2. The name JESUS means _____

3. The name CHRIST means _____

4. The name EMMANUEL means _____

5. Jesus was both true _____ and true _____

6. True or False: Jesus had to be true man so He could take man's place under the Law and suffer and die in his stead.

7. The virgin birth of Jesus is so important because _____

_____

_____

8. True or False: Jesus never hesitated or flinched in dying for us.

9. Jesus was anointed to a threefold office, namely, to be our

_____, _____,

and _____

10. When Jesus said "It is finished!" He meant _____

_____

_____

11. True or False: Jesus descended into hell to suffer.

12. True or False: Jesus redeemed everyone, even those who finally perish.

13. True or False: Jesus came to show us a loving God and that God has nothing against us.

14. True or False: Most ministers and churches do a pretty good job of getting the Good News of Jesus out to their communities.

15. Why did Jesus' enemies seem to repeatedly attack the doctrine of His deity? _____

_____

16. What reason did Jesus have for loving you and saving you?

_____

_____

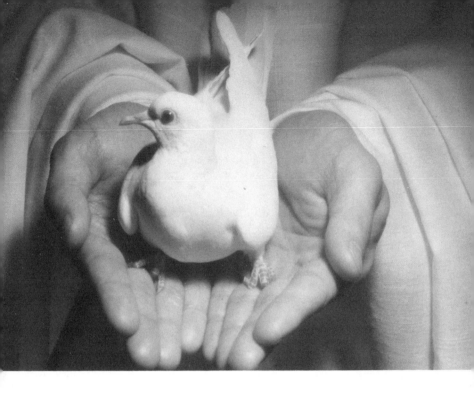

*Lesson 4*

## I HAVE GOOD NEWS FOR YOU

# About A Spirit Who Converts You

### 1. Who is the Holy Spirit?

MATTHEW 28:19 Go and make disciples of all nations, baptizing them in the name of the Father and of the Son *and of the Holy Spirit.*

ACTS 2:1-4 When the day of Pentecost came, they were all together in one place. Suddenly a sound like the *blowing of a violent wind* came from heaven and filled the whole house where they were sitting. They saw what seemed to be *tongues of fire* that separated and came to rest on each of them. All of them were *filled with the Holy Spirit* and began to speak in *other tongues* as the *Spirit enabled them.*

ACTS 5:3-4 Peter said, "Ananias, how is it that Satan has so filled your heart that you have lied to the *Holy Spirit*... You have not lied to men but to *God.*

JOHN 14:16-17 The Father will give you another *Counselor* to be *with you* forever — the *Spirit of truth*... He *lives with you* and will be *in you*.

The Holy Spirit is the third Person of the God-Head. He has other names: Spirit of Truth, Spirit of God, Counselor, and Comforter. He is holy, builds Christ's Church by making people holy (called sanctification), and lives with and in God's people.

## 2. Why is it necessary that the Holy Spirit work saving faith in you?

EPHESIANS 2:1 As for you, *you were dead* in your transgressions and sins.

ROMANS 8:7 The *sinful mind is hostile to God. It does not submit to God's Law, nor can it do so.*

1 CORINTHIANS 2:14 The man without the Spirit *does not accept* the things that come from the Spirit of God, for they are *foolishness* to him, and he *cannot understand* them, because they are spiritually *discerned.*

1 CORINTHIANS 12:3 Therefore I tell you... *no one can say,* "Jesus is Lord," *except by the Holy Spirit.*

By nature we are totally blind to spiritual things. We cannot understand them. We are spiritually dead. We are at war with God. We refuse to do His will. Only the Holy Spirit can restore spiritual life and sight so that we can look at Jesus and honestly say, "He's my Savior!"

## 3. How does the Holy Spirit bring you to faith in Christ?

2 THESSALONIANS 2:13-14 God chose you to be saved *through the*

*sanctifying work of the Spirit* and through belief in the truth. *He called you* to this *through our Gospel.*

ROMANS 10:17   Faith comes from *hearing the message,* and the message is heard through the *word of Christ.*

ROMANS 1:16   I am not ashamed of the *Gospel,* because it is the *power of God* for the *salvation of everyone who believes.*

REVELATION 22:17   The *Spirit* and the Bride say, "*Come!*"

2 CORINTHIANS 4:6   God... *made His light shine* in our *hearts* to give us the light of the *knowledge* of the *glory of God* in the *face of Christ.*

The Holy Spirit calls people to saving faith by the teaching and preaching of the Good News about Jesus. The Holy Spirit uses the Gospel to convert people from spiritual deadness to spiritual life. The Holy Spirit invites and urges the sinner to come. He shines the bright beam of God's love in Jesus into a person's heart where the miracle of new birth or conversion takes place.

## 4. When should you believe in Jesus Christ as Your Savior?

● 2 CORINTHIANS 6:2   I tell you, *now is the time* of God's favor, *now is the day* of salvation.

ISAIAH 55:6   Seek the LORD *while He may be found;* call on Him *while He is near.*

Hell has many citizens who, while on earth, had good intentions. The right time to believe in Jesus is right now while there is time and while the Holy Spirit is working on a person's heart.

## 5. How can you know for sure whether you are converted?

G - od's
R - iches
A - t
C - hrist's
E - xpense

EPHESIANS 2:8-9   It is by *grace* you have been saved, through *faith* — and this not from yourselves, it is

A shy little four year old girl was at the doctor's office for a check-up. The doctor looked in her ear. "Is Big Bird in there?" he asked her. She didn't answer. Then he looked down her throat. "Is Cookie Monster in there?" he asked. Again, no reply. Then he put a stethoscope to her chest. "Is Barney in there?" he asked. She finally spoke and said, "Jesus is in my heart. Barney's on my underwear." How about you? You'll never get close to God unless Jesus is in your heart. Is He there? Are you sure?

the *gift* of God — *not by works,* so that no one can boast.

ACTS 16:29-31  The jailer called for lights, rushed in and *fell trembling* before Paul and Silas. He then brought them out and asked, "Sirs, what must I do to be saved?"   They replied, "*Believe in the Lord Jesus,* and *you will be saved.*"

JOHN 6:47  I tell you the truth, he who *believes has everlasting life.*

A person is converted if he is truly sorry for his sins, trusts not in himself or his good living, but trusts wholly and solely on Jesus Christ for his redemption. He may then know beyond a shadow of a doubt that he is converted, for God has plainly said so in His Word.

## 6.  What else does the Holy Spirit do for you through the Gospel?

ROMANS 15:13  May the God of hope *fill you with all joy and peace* as you trust in Him, so that you may *overflow with hope* by the *power of the Holy Spirit.*

EPHESIANS 2:10  We are God's *workmanship, created* in Christ Jesus to *do good works,* which God *prepared* in advance *for us to do.*

The Holy Spirit gives a believer the fruits of faith, namely: joy, peace, strength to resist sin and power to live a Christian life filled with good works.

## 7.  What is a good work in God's sight?

JOHN 15:5  I am the Vine; you are the branches. If a man *remains in*

*Me* and *I in him,* he will *bear much fruit;* apart from Me *you can do nothing.*

JOHN 14:15  If you love Me, you will *obey what I command.*

HEBREWS 11:6  *Without faith* it is *impossible* to please God.

A good work is whatever God commands people to think, say, or do. This is done out of love for Jesus and by the power of the Holy Spirit.

## 8. Will you stay in your Christian faith? How can you be sure?

1 PETER 1:5  You who through faith are *shielded by God's power.*

1 THESSALONIANS 2:13  God *is at work in you* who believe.

ISAIAH 43:1  Now, this is what the LORD says... "Fear not, for *I have redeemed you; I have summoned you by name; you are Mine.*"

God the Holy Spirit promises to keep the believer in saving faith through the Gospel.

## 9. Does the Holy Spirit desire to do these things for everyone?

EZEKIEL 33:11  *As surely as I live,* declares the Sovereign LORD, I take *no pleasure* in the death of the wicked, but rather that *they turn from their ways and live. Turn! Turn from your evil ways! Why will you die?*

● 1 TIMOTHY 2:4  God *wants all men to be saved* and to come to a *knowledge of the truth.*

Swearing by His very existence, God openly declares that He wants all people to turn from their sins to Jesus and be saved.

## 10. Why, then, are not all people converted?

MATTHEW 23:37   O Jerusalem, Jerusalem, you who kill the prophets and stone those sent to you, how *often* I have *longed to gather* your children together, as a hen gathers her chicks under her wings, but *you were not willing.*

MATTHEW 22:4-6   Tell those who have been invited that I have prepared my dinner: My oxen and fattened cattle have been butchered, and everything is ready. *Come to the wedding banquet.* But *they paid no attention* and went off — one to his field, another to his business. The rest seized his servants, mistreated them and killed them.

ACTS 7:51   You *stiff-necked* people, with *uncircumcised hearts and ears!* You are just like your fathers: *You always resist the Holy Spirit!*

Many people in stubborn unbelief resist the Gospel and the Holy Spirit who strives for their conversion. Whenever a man is brought to saving faith in Jesus it is wholly by God's grace. Whenever a person does not believe and is lost it is wholly his own fault. Those in hell have no excuse.

## Let's pray together

Spirit of Power, Comforter, and Teacher of all spiritual truth, shine into our dark hearts that we may see Jesus. Left to ourselves we would perish in everlasting darkness. Shine into our hearts with the brightness of the Gospel of Christ. Spirit of God, abide with us. Work saving faith in our souls. Give us joy and peace. Keep our faith in Jesus strong, warm and alive. As You moved the early Church to action, so empower and direct us for action-filled lives in the building of Jesus' Church. May we yield ourselves to be Your instruments in bringing the lost to a knowledge of their Savior. May our entire lives be dedicated to this end. And thank You, Holy  Spirit, for teaching us in this Bible study. We praise You. In Jesus' name. Amen.

## Let's sing together

Holy Spirit, light divine. Dawn upon this soul of mine;
Let Your word dispel the night, Wake my spirit, clear my sight.

Holy Spirit, truth divine, Shine upon these eyes of mine;
Send Your radiance from above, Let me know my Savior's love.

Holy Spirit, all divine, Dwell within this self of mine;
I Your temple pure would be Now and for eternity.

## Bible reading schedule for the next seven days

- ❑ 1$^{st}$ day – 1 John 1 & 2
- ❑ 2$^{nd}$ day – 1 John 3 & 4
- ❑ 3$^{rd}$ day – 1 John 5
- ❑ 4$^{th}$ day – Romans 1
- ❑ 5$^{th}$ day – Romans 2
- ❑ 6$^{th}$ day – Romans 3
- ❑ 7$^{th}$ day – Romans 4

## Worksheet no. 4

1. Check the correct statement(s):

   \_\_\_\_\_  The Holy Spirit represents God.

   \_\_\_\_\_  The Holy Spirit is God.

   \_\_\_\_\_  The Holy Spirit speaks for God.

   \_\_\_\_\_  The Holy Spirit does the good works for Christians.

   \_\_\_\_\_  The Father was first in time, then the Son, then the Holy Spirit.

2. Why could you not by your own reason or strength believe in Jesus Christ or come to Him? _____

   _____

3. How many times have you been born? _____

4. True or False: The Holy Spirit alone can convert a person.

5. True or False: When a person is converted we can only conclude that he resisted the Holy Spirit less than those who are not converted.

6. Many people who hear the Gospel are not converted because ( ) they have not had the opportunity to attend a Lutheran Church, ( ) of the devil and his work, ( ) they resisted the Holy Spirit.

7. How long a time does a person have in which to be converted?

   _____

8. Why can't an unbeliever understand spiritual truth by himself?

   _____

9. True or False: A person can know beyond a doubt that he is truly converted.

10. How does the Holy Spirit want to use you to build Christ's Church? _____

    _____

11. A Christian ( ) may do good works, ( ) will do good works, ( ) should do good works.

12. How can a person grieve the Holy Spirit according to Ephesians 4:30-32? _____

13. True or False: According to Romans 8:5-11 we offend the Holy Spirit by resisting His work in us and refusing to do as He prompts us.

14. What are three things the Holy Spirit does for you after conversion?

    a. _____

b. _____

c. _____

15. The _____ is God's power to _____

people. Faith comes from the _____ which

centers in _____. To be God's_____

I must be careful that people hear _____

from me and see _____ in me.

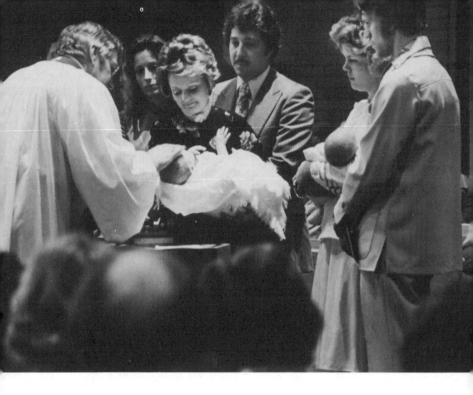

*Lesson 5*

## I HAVE GOOD NEWS FOR YOU

# About A Washing Which
# Cleanses You

### 1. Who commanded baptism?

● MATTHEW 28:18-20 *Jesus* came to them and said, "*All authority* in heaven and on earth has been given to Me. Therefore *go and make disciples of all nations, baptizing* them in the name of the Father and of the Son and of the Holy Spirit, and *teaching* them to obey everything I have commanded you."

Jesus Himself gave us the sacrament of Holy Baptism. Scripture tells how the early Christians happily carried out His command to make disciples of everyone and to baptize them. Note: There are only two Sacraments, that of Baptism and Holy Communion. By a Sacrament we mean a sacred act (1) which was instituted by God, (2) in which there are certain externals such as water, (3) which are united with God's Word, (4) and which offers and conveys the forgiveness of sins and all other spiritual blessings earned by Jesus on the cross.

## 2. What does the word "baptize" mean?

MARK 7:4 When they (the Pharisees and all Jews) come from the marketplace they do not eat unless they *wash* (baptize). And they observe many other traditions, such as the *washing* (baptizing) of cups, pitchers and kettles.

MATTHEW 3:11 I *baptize* you with water for repentance. But after me will come one who... will *baptize* you with the Holy Spirit and with fire.

ACTS 22:16 And now what are you waiting for? Get up, be *baptized* and *wash your sins away,* calling on His name.

MATTHEW 28:19 *Baptize* them *in the name* of the Father and of the Son and of the Holy Spirit.

The Greek word for "baptize" is βαπτιζω (baptizo), which means to wash, pour, or immerse. Some churches believe that a person must be immersed because they think "baptize" means only to immerse. This is incorrect as the passages above indicate. To baptize simply means to apply water whether there are only a few drops or rivers of it. We should not insist that one particular method must be used since God Himself has not done so. The Lord told us to apply water without specifying either the mode or the quantity. The important thing is to use water and God's Word.

**BAPTIZED UNTO THE LORD**

When we are baptized "in the name of the Father and of the Son and of the Holy Spirit," we are brought into union with the one true God. If a person is not baptized in the name of the Holy Trinity (e.g. Unitarian Church), there is no valid baptism.

### 3. Who should administer baptism?

1 CORINTHIANS 4:1 Men ought to regard us as *servants* of Christ and as those *entrusted with the secret things of God.*

Usually pastors administer baptism. You, however, can also baptize, especially in an emergency when one is in danger of death. In the case of older children and adults share the Good News of Jesus' victory over sin and death. Ask the person to confess his sins with you in prayer and embrace Christ as Savior. Then call the person by name, pour or sprinkle water on the person's head and say, "I baptize you in the name of the Father and of the Son and of the Holy Spirit. Amen." If possible, offer a prayer of thanksgiving in your own words and pray the Lord's Prayer.

### 4. Who is to be baptized?

MATTHEW 28:19 Go and make disciples of *all nations, baptizing* them in the name of the Father and of the Son and of the Holy Spirit.

Jesus commands us to baptize all people everywhere, without any distinction of sex or age. All people need to be born again.

### 5. Why should infants be baptized?

MATTHEW 28:19 Go and make disciples of *all nations, baptizing them* in the name of the Father and of the Son and of the Holy Spirit.

ROMANS 3:22-23 There is *no difference,* for *all have sinned* and *fall short* of the glory of God.

PSALM 51:5 *Surely* I was *sinful at birth, sinful from the time my mother conceived me.*

ACTS 2:38-39  Peter replied, "Repent and *be baptized, every one of you,* in the name of Jesus Christ for the *forgiveness of your sins.* And you will *receive the gift of the Holy Spirit.* The promise is for you and your *children* and for *all* who are far off — for *all* whom the Lord our God will call."

JOHN 3:5-7  Jesus answered, "I tell you the truth, *no one can enter* the Kingdom of God *unless he is born of water and the Spirit. Flesh* gives birth to *flesh,* but the *Spirit* gives birth to *spirit.* You should not be surprised at My saying, 'You *must* be born again.'"

MARK 10:13-16  People were bringing *little children* to Jesus to have Him touch them, but the disciples rebuked them. When Jesus saw this, He was indignant. He said to them, "*Let the little children come to Me,* and do not hinder them, for the Kingdom of God *belongs to such as these.* I tell you the truth, anyone who will not *receive* the Kingdom of God *like a little child* will *never* enter it." And He took the children in His arms, put His hands on them and blessed them.

MATTHEW 18:6  If anyone causes one of these *little ones* who *believe in Me* to sin, it would be better for him to have a large millstone hung around his neck and to be drowned in the depths of the sea.

Infants are to be baptized (1) because they are a part of "all nations," (2) because Baptism is the only means by which children can ordinarily be born again, (3) because children also need to receive the Kingdom of God by water and the Spirit just like adults, (4) because they, too, can believe in Jesus as their Savior.

We note that in Baptism God is acting upon man. Only God can give spiritual birth, wash away sin, and give saving faith. No one, young or old, can do this by himself or even help in the process. Many who reject infant Baptism do not understand this. They think one must be older so that he can "understand" the Gospel. "Little children cannot make a decision for Christ," they say. Let us remember, however, that adults cannot do this either. Only God can cause a sinner to believe, and God has also plainly commanded *all* to be baptized. God can do everything on the grand list of Baptismal blessings just as easily for a little child as He can for adults.

To help the baptized person, Sponsors (Godparents) have been introduced. They promise to do all they can to see that the person baptized grows in Christ and good works. They will encourage the baptized person by word, example, and prayer. Only strong Christians should be selected for this important task because only strong Christians can meaningfully promise to do these things.

## 6.  What are the benefits of Baptism?

GALATIANS 3:26-27 You are all sons of God through faith in Christ Jesus, for all of you who were *baptized into Christ* have *clothed yourselves with Christ.*

ACTS 2:38  Repent and *be baptized,* every one of you, in the name of Jesus Christ for the *forgiveness of your sins.* And you will receive the *gift of the Holy Spirit.*

ACTS 22:16 And now what are you waiting for? Get up, be baptized and *wash your sins away,* calling on His name.

MARK 16:16  Whoever believes and is baptized will be *saved.*

1 PETER 3:21  This water (flood and ark) symbolizes *baptism* that now *saves you* also — not the removal of dirt from the body but the pledge of a good conscience toward God. It (baptism) *saves you* by the resurrection of Jesus Christ.

TITUS 3:5  He *saved us through the washing of rebirth* and *renewal by the Holy Spirit.*

JOHN 3:5  Jesus answered, "I tell you the truth, no one can enter the Kingdom of God *unless he is born of water and the Spirit.*"

ACTS 8:35-39 Philip... told him the good news about Jesus. As they traveled along the road, they came to some water and the eunuch said, "Look, here is water. Why shouldn't I be baptized?" Philip said, *"If you believe with all your heart,* you may." The official answered, *"I believe that Jesus Christ is the Son of God."* And he gave orders to stop the chariot. Then both Philip and the eunuch went down into the water and Philip baptized him. When they came up out of the water, the Spirit of the Lord suddenly took Philip away, and the eunuch did not see him again, but *went on his way rejoicing.*

Baptism is more than a symbolic act. It is a real means of grace by which the Holy Spirit causes the sinner and the Savior to be joined, gives forgiveness of sins, brings salvation, new birth and new life, and fills the believer with heavenly joy. It regenerates infants, creating saving faith which accepts these blessings. It seals salvation for adults who already believe, giving them added assurance of forgiveness and the conviction that they are children of God and heirs of everlasting life.

## 7. How can water do such great things?

EPHESIANS 5:25-26   Christ loved the church and gave Himself up for her to make her holy, cleansing her by the washing with *water through the Word.*

MARK 16:16   Whoever *believes* and is baptized will be saved.

It is clear that just splashing water on a person will not save him. But notice that God's Word is connected to the water. God's Word is all-powerful as seen in the creation story in Genesis 1. Paul says that the Gospel is the dynamite of God to save people. This powerful Word is linked to the water and gives it energizing power. It passes forgiveness, life, and salvation on to the person. And it is faith in Jesus and these promises which accepts these great blessings so they are owned by the individual believer.

## 8. Can anyone be saved without being baptized?

LUKE 7:30 The Pharisees and experts in the law *rejected God's purpose* for themselves, because *they had not been baptized* by John.

LUKE 23:42-43 He (the criminal) said, "Jesus, remember me when you come into Your Kingdom." Jesus answered him, "I tell you the truth, *today you will be with Me in paradise.*"

Suppose a baby of Christian parents dies before Baptism. Suppose a man accepts Jesus as Savior but dies immediately without being baptized. The Bible does not say that all who die without Baptism are lost. Saving faith can exist without Baptism. John the Baptist was filled with the Holy Spirit before his birth. The penitent and believing criminal, though not baptized, went to Paradise. Holy Baptism is necessary. We cannot willfully turn it down and be saved. We are bound to Baptism because God plainly commands it, yet He is not bound as the examples mentioned illustrate.

## 9. What is the significance of Baptism?

GALATIANS 3:26-27 You are all sons of God through faith in Christ Jesus, for all of you who were *baptized into* Christ have *clothed yourselves with Christ.*

ROMANS 6:4 We were therefore *buried with Him through baptism* into death in order that, just as Christ was raised from the dead through the glory of the Father, *we too may live a new life.*

ACTS 8:39 When they came up out of the water, the Spirit of the Lord suddenly took Philip away, and the eunuch did not see him again, but *went on his way rejoicing.*

A person is born once, and Scripture says that all those so born are born to trouble and tears. A person is born a second time, but this time it is to hope, happiness, and heaven. Because Baptism forms a union between a man and his Savior, all the qualities of Christ Himself are bestowed upon the man. He shares in Jesus' burial, in His death, and in His resurrection. He is encouraged to shun sin and serve God with a Christian life. Whether Baptism is the cause of salvation such as in infants or a seal of salvation to others, there is new life and joy. Praise be to the Lord who earned it all for us by His suffering, death, and resurrection!

## Let's pray together

Dear God, thank You for this instruction on Holy Baptism. Forgive us for our misconceptions and frequent lack of faith in this washing and the blessings You would bring us. Give to us and to those still in spiritual darkness new birth through water and the Holy Spirit. Take away our sins for Jesus' sake. Keep us ever mindful of how our blessed Lord suffered and died on the Cross for our redemption. Help us remember our own Baptism and the blessings which are ours through it. May our Baptismal joy and strength be great. And finally, may we do all in our power to make disciples of all people by witnessing and baptizing. In Jesus' name. Amen.

## Let's sing together

> Rock of Ages, cleft for me,
> Let me hide myself in Thee;
> Let the water and the blood
> From Thy riven side which flowed
> Be of sin the double cure,
> Cleanse me from its guilt and pow'r.
>
> Not the labors of my hands
> Can fulfill Thy Law's demands;
> Could my zeal no respite know,
> Could my tears forever flow,
> All for sin could not atone;
> Thou must save, and Thou alone.
>
> Nothing in my hand I bring,
> Simply to Thy cross I cling;
> Naked, come to Thee for dress;
> Helpless, look to Thee for grace;

Foul, I to the fountain fly —
Wash me, Savior, or I die!

## Bible reading schedule for next seven days

- ❏ 1ˢᵗ day – Romans 5
- ❏ 2ⁿᵈ day – Romans 6
- ❏ 3ʳᵈ day – Romans 7
- ❏ 4ᵗʰ day – Romans 8

- ❏ 5ᵗʰ day – Romans 9
- ❏ 6ᵗʰ day – Romans 10
- ❏ 7ᵗʰ day – Romans 11

## Worksheet no. 5

1. Prove with a Bible passage from this Lesson that we are to baptize and teach everyone: _____

2. Why is it so important that after Baptism we also teach them?

_____

_____

3. An act is a Sacrament when it:

   a. _____

   b. _____

   c. _____

   d. _____

4. To perform a valid Baptism one must:

   _____ Tell the person the Gospel story.

   _____ Ask the person if he believes it.

   _____ Have a prayer and the confession of sins.

   _____ Call the person by name.

   _____ Apply water to the person.

   _____ Say, "I baptize you in the name of the Father and of the

Son and of the Holy Spirit. Amen."

5. We may baptize by (   ) sprinkling, (   ) pouring, (   ) immersing.

6. Why do some churches reject infant Baptism? _____

_____

_____

7. True or False: The Bible does not command us to baptize infants.

8. True or False: Every baptized person receives forgiveness of sins.

9. True or False: Baptism is more than a symbol; it also brings salvation. A Bible verse which proves it: _____

10. True or False: Baptism is no more than a symbol on the part of the baptized person that through faith in Christ he has forgiveness of sins.

11. True or False: When the Bible says that Baptism saves us, this is a contradiction of other passages which say that Christ alone saves us.

12. What gives power to the water in Baptism? _____

_____

13. Briefly explain the statement: "Baptism is a means of grace."

_____

_____

14. According to Matthew 28:18-20 there are two ways we can make Christians out of people and that is by _____

15. What practical meaning should your Baptism have for you in your daily life? _____

_____

_____

*Lesson 6*

## I HAVE GOOD NEWS FOR YOU

# About A Meal Which Feeds You

### 1. What is the Lord's Supper?

MATTHEW 26:26-28, MARK 14:22-24, LUKE 22:19,20, 1 CORINTHIANS
11:23-25  The Lord Jesus, on the night He was betrayed, took
bread, and when He had given thanks, He broke it, and gave it to
His disciples, saying, "Take and eat. *This is My body*, which is given
for you. Do this in remembrance of Me." In the same way He also
took the cup after supper, and when He had given thanks, He gave
it to them, saying, "Drink from it, all of you. *This is My blood* of the
new covenant which is poured out for many for the forgiveness of
sins. *Do this*, whenever you drink it, *in remembrance of Me.*"

 On Maundy Thursday, only hours before His betrayal by Judas and His death on the cross, Jesus was gathered with His disciples in an upper room in Jerusalem to celebrate the Passover (Exodus 12:1-14). A new and better Meal was about to replace the old Passover meal. It would be only for disciples of Jesus who were to celebrate it often in remembrance of Him. Beside bread and wine Christians also eat and drink Christ's body and blood. We cannot fathom this mystery, but we know that His words are true, and we believe them.

Other names for the Lord's Supper are **HOLY COMMUNION** — reminding us of the union of the elements and the union of believers with their Lord and with each other, **LORD'S TABLE** — reminding us that it is set by the Lord with heavenly food, **SACRAMENT OF THE ALTAR** — reminding us that it is usually celebrated at an altar in God's House, **BREAKING OF BREAD** — reminding us that the loaves were broken into smaller pieces by our Lord and were then handed to His followers, and **EUCHARIST** — giving of thanks.

## 2.  What is present at the Lord's Table?

MATTHEW 26:26-28  While they were eating, Jesus took bread, gave thanks and broke it, and gave it to His disciples, saying, "Take and eat; *this is My body.*" Then He took the *cup*, gave thanks and offered it to them, saying, "Drink from it, all of you. *This is My blood* of the covenant, which is poured out for many for the forgiveness of sins."

1 CORINTHIANS 10:15-16  I speak to sensible people; judge for yourselves what I say. *Is not the cup* of thanksgiving for which we give thanks *a participation in the blood of Christ?* And *is not the bread* that we break *a participation in the body of Christ?*

1 CORINTHIANS 11:26-28  For whenever you eat this *bread* and drink this *cup*, you proclaim the Lord's death until He comes. Therefore,

whoever eats the *bread* or drinks the *cup* of the Lord in an unworthy manner will be guilty of sinning against the *body and blood of the Lord.* A man ought to examine himself before he eats of the *bread* and drinks of the *cup.*

In the bread and wine Jesus is present both as the Giver and the Gift. His simple promise is that when we eat the bread we also truly receive His body, and when we drink from the cup we truly receive His blood. We may refer to this as the real presence of Christ's body and blood in the Lord's Supper.

Some churches do not believe that the bread and body and the wine and blood are together in this Meal. The Catholic Church believes that after consecration the bread has been totally changed into the body of Christ and the wine into His blood (transubstantiation) so that only two elements are received by the communicant. Most reformed churches, however, believe that Christ's body and blood are not present. "He is in heaven," they say. "The communicant receives only the bread and wine (or grape juice) which are symbols or representations of His body and blood."

But this is not what Jesus says. Jesus says that the bread "is" His body. "Is" does not mean "symbolizes" or "represents." Furthermore, Paul says all four elements — bread, wine, body, and blood — are in the Lord's Supper. It is important to believe just what God's Word says. This is a powerful meal. It is a high calorie spiritual food earned by the Lord on the Cross and set with rich blessings, forgiveness of sins, joy and peace, for all His children to take and make their own.

## 3. What are the purposes and benefits of the Lord's Supper?

LUKE 22:19-20  And He took bread, gave thanks and broke it, and gave it to them, saying, "This is My body given *for you*; do this in *remembrance of Me.*" In the same way, after the supper He took the cup, saying, "This cup is the *new covenant* in My blood, which is poured out *for you*."

MATTHEW 26:27-28  Then He took the cup, gave thanks and offered it to them, saying, "Drink from it, all of you. This is My blood of the *covenant,* which is poured out for many for the *forgiveness of sins*."

1 CORINTHIANS 11:26  Whenever you eat this bread and drink this cup, *you proclaim the Lord's death* until he comes.

1 CORINTHIANS 10:17  Because there is one loaf, *we*, who are many, *are one body,* for we all partake of the one loaf.

The purpose of this meal is to give us the most personal assurance that our sins are forgiven through faith in Jesus; it is a covenant or promise by the Lord. By it we receive strength and encouragement to live a holier, more dedicated life. We remember Jesus' death which gives us life and forgiveness of sins. When we go to the Lord's Table we publicly preach a powerful sermon: the theme — Jesus gave His body and shed His blood to make atonement for our sins! We also proclaim that we are one with Jesus and with each other. When this Table is set, Jesus is saying, "Come and help yourself. It's all for you!"

### 4. Does everyone who attends the Lord's Supper automatically receive these blessings?

1 CORINTHIANS 11:27,29-30  Whoever eats the bread or drinks the cup of the Lord in an *unworthy manner* will be *guilty of sinning* against the body and blood of the Lord... For anyone who eats and drinks *without recognizing* the body of the Lord *eats and drinks judgment on himself.* That is why many among you are weak and sick, and a number of you have fallen asleep.

HEBREWS 11:6  Without *faith* it is impossible to please God.

In and of themselves no person is worthy of the Lord's Supper, no one except he who believes on the Lord Jesus. Christ makes us worthy. Those who do not believe that Jesus died to save them or who do not believe that His body and blood are present in the Supper bring judgment on themselves.

## 5. Who should not eat and drink the Lord's Supper?

1 CORINTHIANS 11:28-29 A man ought to *examine himself before* he eats of the bread and drinks of the cup. For anyone who eats and drinks *without recognizing* the body of the Lord eats and drinks judgment on himself.

1 CORINTHIANS 10:21 You *cannot* drink the *cup of the Lord and the cup of demons too*; you *cannot* have a part in *both the Lord's table and the table of demons.*

ACTS 2:42 They (the early Christians) *devoted* themselves to the apostles' *teaching* and to the *fellowship*, to the *breaking of bread* and to *prayer.*

MATTHEW 5:23-24 If you are offering your gift at the altar and there remember that your brother has something against you, *leave your gift* there in front of the altar. *First go and be reconciled* to your brother; *then come and offer* your gift.

ROMANS 16:17 I urge you, brothers, to watch out for those who *cause divisions and put obstacles* in your way that are contrary to the teaching you have learned. *Keep away from them.*

These people should not eat and drink the Lord's Supper: (1) Those who do not believe in Jesus and who really want to serve the devil, (2) Those who cannot examine themselves properly or who do not see the Lord's body and blood in the bread and wine, (3) Those who have offended someone and forgiveness is not given, (4) Those who do not believe the teachings of the apostles because Communion is an expression of our oneness.

## 6. How should I prepare for the Lord's Supper?

1 CORINTHIANS 11:28-29,31  A man ought to *examine himself* before he eats of the bread and drinks of the cup. For anyone who eats and drinks without *recognizing* the body of the Lord eats and drinks judgment on himself... But if we *judged ourselves*, we would not come under judgment.

PSALM 51:17  The sacrifices of God are a *broken spirit*, a *broken and contrite heart*, O God, You will not despise.

MARK 1:15 "The time has come," Jesus said. "The Kingdom of God is near. *Repent* and *believe* the Good News!"

PSALM 119:32  I *run in the path* of Your commands, for *You have set my heart free.*

Before going to the Lord's Supper we should carefully examine our hearts. Do we recognize His body and blood in the bread and wine? Are we sorry for our sins? Do we have a desire to turn away from our pet sins? Do we really believe the Good News of Jesus' victory over sin and death on the Cross for us?

## 7. Should we attend the Table if we have sinned or if we have a weak faith?

MARK 9:23-24,26 Jesus said, "Everything is possible for him who believes." Immediately the boy's father exclaimed, "I do believe; help me overcome my *unbelief!*"... The spirit shrieked, convulsed him violently and *came out.*

ISAIAH 42:3  A *bruised reed* He will not break, and a *smoldering wick* He will *not snuff out.*

● JOHN 6:37  *Whoever comes* to Me *I will never drive away.*

A father brought his possessed and epileptic son to Jesus for healing. His faith was weak, but the Lord healed his son. A broken plant is tied up to save it, and the smoking wick is given oil and trimmed so it may burn brightly. We should always come to Jesus even though we have sinned, have a weak faith, or are discouraged. We should come to the Lord's Supper even at these times. The Lord will always warmly receive, forgive, and strengthen us. Friedrich C. Heyder wrote —

*I come, O Savior, to Your table, For weak and weary is my soul;*
*You Bread of Life, alone are able To satisfy and make me whole.*
*Lord, may Your body and Your blood Be for my soul the highest good!*

## 8. Why should we receive the Lord's Supper frequently?

1 CORINTHIANS 11:25-26 "*Do this*, whenever you drink it, *in remembrance of Me.*" For whenever you eat this bread and drink this cup, you *proclaim the Lord's death until He comes.*

LUKE 22:19-20 "This is My body given *for you; do this in remembrance of* Me"... "This cup is the new covenant in My blood, which is *poured out for you.*"

MATTHEW 26:27-28 Jesus said, "*Drink from it, all of you.* This is My blood of the covenant, which is poured out for many *for the forgiveness of sins.*"

● MATTHEW 11:28 *Come to Me*, all you who are *weary and burdened,* and *I will give you rest.*

We should come to the Lord's Supper often because Jesus told us to do so in memory of Him, so that we may frequently proclaim His death, so that we may have added assurance that all our sins are forgiven, and so that we may have spiritual rest and strength.

## Let's pray together

Dear Lord, thank You for instituting this sacred meal which we have just studied. In the bread and wine You are present with Your body and blood. Keep us from impenitence and unbelief, from not being reconciled to others, or from any other sin which would keep us from this blessed Supper. Instead, may we come to eat and drink even though our faith may be weak or though we may have sinned grievously against You. As we come may we be assured by You that our sins are completely forgiven. Give us joy, peace, and strength. Then we shall have power to live for You, to spend ourselves in building Your Kingdom, and to be Your instruments in bringing many others to believe in You. This shall be our life's work until You call us to be guests with You at Your heavenly table — there we will forever thank You for Your unspeakable mercy and grace to us. Amen.

## Let's sing together

> I come, O Savior to Your Table,
> For weak and weary is my soul;
> You, Bread of Life, alone are able
> To satisfy and make me whole.
> Lord, may Your body and Your blood
> Be for my soul the highest good.
>
> Your body crucified, O Savior,
> Your blood which once for me was shed,
> These are my life and strength forever,
> By them my hungry soul is fed.
> Lord, may Your body and Your blood
> Be for my soul the highest good.
>
> My heart has now become Your dwelling,
> O blessed, holy Trinity.
> With angels I, Your praises telling,
> Shall live in joy eternally.
> Lord, may Your body and Your blood
> Be for my soul the highest good.

## Bible reading schedule for the next seven days

❏ 1st day – Romans 12          ❏ 5th day – Romans 16
❏ 2nd day – Romans 13          ❏ 6th day – Acts 1
❏ 3rd day – Romans 14          ❏ 7th day – Acts 2

❑  4th day – Romans 15

## Worksheet no. 6

1. Jesus instituted the Lord's Supper on (   ) Epiphany, (   ) Ash Wednesday, (   ) Pentecost, (   ) Maundy Thursday.

2. When Jesus instituted the Lord's Supper, which Old Testament festival was He observing? (   ) Pentecost, (   ) The Day of Atonement, (   ) The Passover.

3. Check the correct statement(s):

   __ Christ's body and blood are present in the bread and wine.

   __ Only believers receive Jesus' body and blood in Holy Communion.

   __ Everyone who eat and drinks does so to his salvation.

   __ Like medicine is for the sick so Communion is for sinners.

4. What elements does the communicant receive when attending the Lord's Table:

   a. According to Catholic beliefs? _____

   b. According to many reformed churches? _____

   c. According to the Bible? _____

5. How is the Lord's Supper like Memorial Day? _____

   _____

   _____

6. True or False: Before going to Communion we must prove that we are worthy of it.

7. True or False: Only Lutherans and members of the con-

gregation can be permitted to go to Communion.

8. Before eating and drinking Paul tells us to examine ourselves. What are three appropriate questions we should ask ourselves?

   a. _____

   b. _____

   c. _____

9. True or False: The frequency of our Communion attendance should be determined by our feelings. Generally speaking we should attend Communion only when we feel a need for it.

10. True or False: The Lord's Supper might become meaningless to us if we attend too often. Almost anything can be overdone.

11. List at least three purposes of the Lord's Supper:

    a. _____

    b. _____

    c. _____

12. What is significant about the term, Holy COMMUNION?

    _____

    _____

    _____

13. When going to the Lord's Table we are to do it in remembrance of Jesus. What should we remember? _____

    _____

    _____

*Lesson 7*

# I HAVE GOOD NEWS FOR YOU

# About A Devotional Life
## Which Blesses You

### 1. What are some of the privileges and benefits of public worship?

ECCLESIASTES 5:1  *Guard your steps* when you go to the house of God. *Go near to listen* rather than to offer the *sacrifice of fools*, who *do not know that they do wrong.*

PSALM 26:8  I *love* the house *where You live*, O LORD,  the place where *Your glory dwells.*

PSALM 27:4 *One thing I ask* of the LORD, *this is what I seek:* that I may *dwell in the house of the LORD* all the days of my life, to *gaze upon the beauty* of the LORD and *to seek Him* in His temple.

2 CHRONICLES 30:8    Do not be stiff-necked, as your fathers were; *submit* to the LORD. *Come* to the sanctuary, which He has consecrated forever. *Serve* the LORD your God, so that His fierce anger will turn away from you.

LUKE 10:39-42  Martha had a sister called Mary, who sat at the Lord's feet *listening to what He said.* But *Martha was distracted* by all the preparations that had to be made. She came to Him and asked, "Lord, don't you care that my sister has left me to do the work by myself? Tell her to help me!" "Martha, Martha," the Lord answered, "you are *worried and upset about many things,* but *only one thing is needed.* Mary has *chosen what is better,* and it *will not be taken away* from her."

● ROMANS 10:17  Consequently, *faith comes from hearing the message,* and the *message is heard through the word of Christ.*

PSALM 122:1  I (David) *rejoiced* with those who said to me, "Let us go to the house of the LORD."

It is a great privilege to come into God's presence in public worship. He tells us to watch our steps as we go to meet Him, to come close to Him to better see His beauty, to listen to His counsel, and to praise Him in word and song. In worship we are personally involved with God and He with us. We are also in fellowship with other members of God's family. Here we give and receive mutual encouragement and experience spiritual growth which brings glory to God.

## 2.  What role should Bible study groups, family and private devotions play in my life?

HEBREWS 10:25 Let us not give up *meeting together,* as some are in the habit of doing, but let us *encourage one another* — and all the more as you see the Day approaching.

ACTS 2:42 They (the early Christians) *devoted themselves* to the *apostles' teaching* and to the *fellowship,* to the *breaking of bread* and to *prayer.*

ACTS 20:7,9-12 *On the first day of the week we came together* to break bread. *Paul spoke* to the people and, because he intended to leave the next day, kept on talking until midnight... Seated in a window was a young man named Eutychus, who was *sinking into a deep sleep* as Paul talked on and on. When he was *sound asleep,* he fell to the ground from the third story and was picked up dead. Paul went down, threw himself on the young man and put his arms around him. "Don't be alarmed," he said. "He's alive!" Then he went upstairs again and broke bread and ate. After talking until daylight, he left. The people took the young man home alive and were *greatly comforted.*

COLOSSIANS 3:16 Let the *Word* of Christ *dwell in you richly* as you *teach and admonish* one another with all *wisdom,* and as you *sing psalms, hymns and spiritual songs* with *gratitude in your hearts to God.*

● LUKE 11:28 Jesus replied, "*Blessed* rather are those who *hear* the Word of God and *obey* it."

ACTS 17:11 Now the Bereans... received the message with *great eagerness* and *examined* the Scriptures *every day* to see if what Paul said was true.

Most early Christians were excited about studying Holy Scripture. They were convinced it was the very Word of God. We should follow their example. The time spent in Bible study groups brings spiritual growth, encouragement, and good fellowship.

It is also important to have daily Bible study at home alone and with a family where possible. Some important suggestions to make your daily Bible study a success: (1) Beside your Bible have a good devotional book to assist you (ask your pastor for suggestions). (2) Have Bible study at the same time each day. Many believers do this after the evening meal, others before bedtime, and some at breakfast. Always have devotions, even when there is company or when out of town. Never, never skip. (3) Ask what the Lord is really trying to say to you in the study, and then, have a prayer to Him to drive it home. You will know the joy and power of the Lord's presence in your life on daily basis (Deuteronomy 6:6,7; Psalm 19:10; Jeremiah 15:16).

### 3.  What is prayer?

PSALM 19:14  May the *words of my mouth* and the *meditation of my heart* be pleasing in Your sight, O LORD, my Rock and my Redeemer.

PSALM 10:17  You hear, O LORD, the *desire* of the afflicted; You encourage them, and You listen to their cry.

Prayer is having a talk with God. We share with God our thoughts, joys, and sorrows aloud or just from the heart. Annie Hawks and Robert Lowry wrote:

> *Prayer is the Christian's vital breath, The Christian's native air,*
> *His watchword at the gates of death: He enters heaven with prayer.*
>
> *O Lord, by whom we come to God, The Life, the Truth, the Way,*
> *The path of prayer Thyself hast trod: Lord, teach us how to pray.*

### 4.  What are some important qualities of prayer?

MATTHEW 4:10  Jesus said... it is written: "*Worship* the Lord your God, and serve Him *only.* "

JOHN 16:23-24 Jesus said... I tell you the truth, My Father will give you whatever you *ask in My name*. Until now you have not asked for anything in My name. Ask and you *will receive*, and your *joy will be complete*.

ISAIAH 63:16 But You are our Father, though *Abraham does not know us* or *Israel (Jacob) acknowledge us; You*, O LORD, *are our Father*, our Redeemer from of old is Your name.

JAMES 1:6-7 When he asks, he must *believe* and *not doubt*, because he who doubts is like a wave of the sea, blown and tossed by the wind. That man *should not think* he will receive anything from the Lord.

MATTHEW 6:7-8 When you pray, *do not keep on babbling* like pagans, for they think they will be heard because of their *many words*. Do not be like them, for your Father *knows what you need before you ask Him*.

1 JOHN 5:14 This is the *confidence* we have in approaching God: that if we ask anything *according to His will, He hears us*.

We must pray to the one true God, Father, Son, and Holy Spirit. All prayers to other gods are false and not heard. We can talk to God only through our Lord Jesus. We must believe that God hears our prayers and can answer them. Lengthy prayers are not necessary. It is God's will to give us all manner of spiritual gifts, and so we pray unconditionally. When praying for physical blessings we add, "If it be Your will!" We will let God decide to give us these things or not.

## 5.  What else does the Bible tell us about prayer?

1 TIMOTHY 2:1-2 I urge, then, first of all, that *requests, prayers, intercession and thanksgiving* be made for everyone — for kings and all those in authority, that we may live peaceful and quiet lives in all godliness and holiness.

MATTHEW 5:43-44 You have heard that it was said, "Love your neighbor and hate your enemy." But I tell you: Love your enemies

and *pray for those who persecute you.*

PSALM 50:15   *Call* upon Me in the day of trouble; I will *deliver* you, and you will *honor* Me.

1 THESSALONIANS 5:16-18   Be joyful always; *pray continually; give thanks in all circumstances,* for this is *God's will for you* in Christ Jesus.

PHILIPPIANS 4:6   *Do not be anxious about anything,* but *in everything,* by *prayer* and *petition,* with *thanksgiving, present your requests* to God.

HEBREWS 9:27   Man is destined to die once, and *after that to face judgment.*

MATTHEW 6:5-6   When you pray, do not be like the hypocrites, for they love to pray standing in the synagogues and on the street corners to be *seen by men.* I tell you the truth, *they have received their reward in full.* But when you pray, *go into your room, close the door* and pray to your Father, who is unseen. Then *your Father, who sees what is done in secret, will reward you.*

ISAIAH 65:24   *Before they call* I *will answer,* while they are *still speaking* I *will hear.*

We pray because (1) God invites us to, (2) God promises to hear us, (3) of our own needs and those of others, and (4) of gratitude for all blessings received. We should pray for everyone, even our enemies. We should pray when we have trouble. God promises to help us. We should then thank Him. We should not pray for or to the dead, nor should we make a show of our prayer life. God answers prayer in one of three ways: (1) No! (2) Yes! (3) Wait!

## 6.  How does Jesus teach us to pray?

MATTHEW 6:9-13; LUKE 11:2-4   This is how you should pray: Our Father in heaven, hallowed be Your name, Your Kingdom come,

Your will be done on earth as it is in heaven. Give us today our daily bread. Forgive us our sins, as we also forgive those who sin against us. Lead us not into temptation, but deliver us from evil. For the Kingdom, the power, and the glory are Yours now and forever. Amen.

## INTRODUCTION

**"Our Father in heaven"**: Jesus teaches us to call God our "Father." The word "Father" should inspire full trust in Him. We are His children. As little children trust and speak to their earthly father, so we trust and speak to our Father in heaven.

## SPIRITUAL BLESSINGS

**"Hallowed be Your name"**: Hallow means holy. God's name is holy by itself. Here we pray that God's name will be holy to us, that we will love, honor, glorify, and trust Him in our thoughts, words, and actions. In these ways we show that God's name is holy to us.

**"Your Kingdom come"**: This means: Father, may Your Kingdom grow in my heart, my home, my church, my country, and in all the world. Here we promise God that we will help build His Kingdom. We will be fishers of men. No matter who we are or where we are, at home, at work, in school, on vacation — the Kingdom of God is first, and we will personally do all we can to help it grow.

**"Your will be done on earth as it is in heaven"**: We are asking that God's will be done as perfectly on earth as it is done in heaven. We ask God to have His will done among us and by us.

## BODILY BLESSINGS

**"Give us today our daily bread"**: Daily bread means everything we need for life — food, clothing, home, good government, good weather, employment, health — everything that makes our lives happy and successful. All these are gifts from God.

## TURNING AWAY FROM EVIL

**"Forgive us our sins, as we also forgive those who sin against us"**: We are asking God to forgive us as we forgive others. We receive God's full, free forgiveness because of Jesus Christ. We will now forgive others who sin against us.

**"Lead us not into temptation"**: God does not tempt people to sin. Here we pray that God will protect us so that the devil, the world, and our own flesh will not fool us or lead us to sin or to stop believing in Jesus. In this way we overcome and win spiritual victories.

**"But deliver us from evil"**: There is evil all around us. Here we pray that God will shield us from evil. If God permits a burden to come, we ask Him to give us strength to bear it. When life is over, we ask God to take us to our new home in heaven where there will be no evil.

## CONCLUSION

**"For the Kingdom, the power, and the glory are Yours now and forever"**: This is a wonderful way to end a wonderful prayer. Our Father in heaven has all power. He can do whatever He promises. He will do everything He promises. And He has promised us much. We are completely safe in His hands. We also promise God that we will continue to give Him all glory now and forever in heaven.

**"Amen"**: This word means "it shall be so" or "so let it be."

### Let's pray together

Heavenly Father, we give You all praise for the Scriptures we have just studied. May we use every opportunity we have to worship You in public worship services with other believers. May we study Your Word and fellowship with You and fellow believers in Bible study groups, in daily family devotions, and daily private study. Forgive us for the times when we worshiped or prayed thoughtlessly or mechanically. Please richly bless our prayer life. Move us to come to You with our troubles and our sins. Then You will receive honor, and we will be happy. We ask this in the name of Jesus Christ who Himself spent many a night in prayer. Amen.

## Let's sing together

What a Friend we have in Jesus, All our sins and griefs to bear!
What a privilege to carry Ev'rything to God in prayer!
Oh, what peace we often forfeit, Oh, what needless pain we bear,
All because we do not carry Ev'rything to God in prayer!

Have we trials and temptations? Is there trouble anywhere?
We should never be discouraged, Take it to the Lord in prayer.
Can we find a Friend so faithful Who will all our sorrows share?
Jesus knows our ev'ry weakness — Take it to the Lord in prayer.

Are we weak and heavy laden, Cumbered with a load of care?
Precious Savior, still our Refuge — Take it to the Lord in prayer.
Do your friends despise, forsake You? Take it to the Lord in prayer;
In His arms He'll take and shield you, You will find a solace there.

## Bible reading schedule for the next seven days

❑ 1st day – Acts 3
❑ 2nd day – Acts 4
❑ 3rd day – Acts 5
❑ 4th day – Acts 6
❑ 5th day – Acts 7
❑ 6th day – Acts 8
❑ 7th day – Acts 9

## Worksheet no. 7

1. True or False: People who say they worship God out in the woods on Sunday morning or the golf course instead of church usually do.

2. What does public worship offer that private worship does not?

3. What does group Bible study offer that public worship does not? _____

4. Why is it important for you to have family or personal devotions in your home each day? _____

_____

5. On a scale of 1 – 10 where were you spiritually five years ago? _____. A year ago? _____. Today? _____. What does this tell you about your devotional life? _____

_____

6. When praying for physical blessings we should always add ___

_____

7. True or False: When we pray we have as many reasons to thank God for the things He does not give us as for the things He does give us.

8. How do we hallow God's name? _____

_____

9. What do we mean when we pray, "Your Kingdom come"? ___

_____

_____

10. True or False: Forgiven of all our sins we promise God that we will, if possible, forgive those who sin against us.

11. Four basic reasons why we pray are:

a. _____

b. _____

c. _____

d. _____

12. If God already knows all about our needs even before we ask Him, why ask? _____

_____

13. True or False: God always answers prayer.

14. Write out a mealtime prayer: _____

_____

_____

_____

15. What does "Amen" mean? _____

_____

*Lesson 8*

# I HAVE GOOD NEWS FOR YOU

# About Keys Which Lock and Unlock

## 1. What is the Church of Jesus Christ?

EPHESIANS 2:19-21 You are *no longer foreigners* and *aliens,* but *fellow citizens with God's people* and *members of God's household,* built on the *foundation of the apostles and prophets,* with *Christ Jesus* Himself as the *chief cornerstone.* In Him the *whole building is joined together* and *rises to become a holy temple* in the Lord.

ROMANS 12:5 In Christ *we who are many form one body,* and *each member belongs to all the others.*

ROMANS 8:9 If anyone does *not have the Spirit of Christ,* he *does not belong to Christ.*

LUKE 17:20-21  The Kingdom of God does not come with your *careful observation,* nor will people say, "Here it is," or "There it is," because the *Kingdom of God is within you.*

2 TIMOTHY 2:19  The *Lord knows* those who are His.

EPHESIANS 5:25-27  Christ loved the church and gave Himself up for her to make her *holy, cleansing her* by the washing with water through the Word, and to *present her to Himself* as a *radiant* church, *without stain or wrinkle* or any other *blemish,* but *holy* and *blameless.*

1 PETER 2:5  You also, like *living stones,* are *being built* into a *spiritual house* to be a *holy priesthood, offering spiritual sacrifices* acceptable to God through Jesus Christ.

● 1 CORINTHIANS 3:11  For no one can lay *any foundation other than* the one already laid, which is *Jesus Christ.*

There is only one true Church of Jesus Christ that will last forever, and it is to be distinguished from denominations and congregations. It is made up of all true believers who are members of God's family. These believers are built together on Christ, the Cornerstone of the Church. Hypocrites and godless people do not belong. We cannot see the true Church because the Church resides in each believer's heart. This Church is clean, pure and has no fault; it has been cleansed by the blood of Jesus. The believers in this Church are living stones. They serve God as holy priests and offer many good works acceptable to God through Jesus.

## 2. What are the keys to the Kingdom?

MATTHEW 16:19  I will give you the *Keys of the Kingdom of Heaven*; whatever you *bind* on earth will be *bound* in heaven, and whatever you *loose* on earth will be *loosed* in heaven.

MARK 16:15 Jesus said to them, "*Go* into all the world and *preach the Good News* to all creation."

MATTHEW 28:18-20 Jesus came to them and said, "*All authority* in heaven and on earth has been given to Me. Therefore *go and make disciples* of all nations, *baptizing them* in the name of the Father and of the Son and of the Holy Spirit, and *teaching them* to obey everything I have commanded you."

JOHN 20:22-23 Jesus breathed on them and said, "Receive the Holy Spirit. *If you forgive* anyone his sins, *they are forgiven*; if you *do not forgive* them, *they are not forgiven*."

Jesus wants us to make disciples of all people. A disciple is: (1) A student of the Master, (2) A follower of the Master, and (3) One who makes disciples of others for the Master. The Lord gives to all believers on earth the Keys of the Kingdom, namely, the authority and power to tell the Good News, to baptize and serve the Lord's Supper, and to forgive or not forgive sins. Daniel March put it well:

> *Let none hear you idly saying, "There is nothing I can do, "*
> *While the multitudes are dying And the Master calls for you.*
> *Take the task He gives you gladly; Let His work your pleasure be.*
> *Answer quickly when He calls you, "Here am I. Send me, send me!"*

## 3. To whom has the Lord given these keys?

MATTHEW 16:19 "*I will give you the Keys* of the Kingdom of Heaven; *whatever you bind* on earth will be bound in heaven, and *whatever you loose* on earth will be loosed in heaven" (To Peter as the spokesman of the disciples).

JOHN 20:22-23 Jesus breathed on *them* and said, "Receive the Holy Spirit. If *you* forgive anyone his sins, they are forgiven; if *you* do not forgive them, they are not forgiven."

1 PETER 2:9 *You* are a chosen people, a *royal priesthood*, a holy nation, a people belonging to God, *that you may declare the praises of Him* who called you out of darkness into His wonderful light.

MATTHEW 18:17-18,20 If he refuses to listen to them, tell it to the *church*; and if he refuses to listen even to the church, treat him as you would a pagan or a tax collector. I tell you the truth, *whatever you bind* on earth will be bound in heaven, and *whatever you loose* on earth will be loosed in heaven. For where *two or three come together in My name, there am I with them.*

> What is the Church to me?
> The Church to me my joy shall be —
>    A house to build, a name to bear,
> A fellowship both strong and fair,
> An influence to spread abroad
> That men may know the Son of God.
> Such offering to Him I bring
>    Who is the Church's Lord and King
> And Savior unto me.
>
> by Margaret Seebach

The Lord has given these Keys to all Christians on earth individually and as they are gathered together in local congregations in His name.

## 4. Whose sins are forgiven and whose sins are not forgiven?

ACTS 3:19 *Repent,* then, and *turn* to God, so that your sins may be wiped out, that *times of refreshing* may come from the Lord.

PSALM 51:17 My sacrifice, O God, is a *broken spirit;* a *broken* and *contrite heart,* O God, You will not despise.

2 SAMUEL 12:13 David said to Nathan, "*I have sinned against the LORD.*" Nathan replied, "*The LORD has taken away your sin. You are not going to die.*"

● MARK 16:16 Whoever *believes and is baptized* will be *saved,* but whoever *does not believe will be condemned.*

We should announce forgiveness and God's eternal love to all who repent and are sorry for their sins, who desire to turn away from them, and who believe in Jesus Christ as their personal Savior from their sins. We should tell people who refuse God's love in Christ that their sins are not forgiven. We continue to love them and urge them to see their sin and their Savior so that they may be saved.

## 5.  What about church discipline and excommunication?

1 CORINTHIANS 5:12-13  What business is it of mine to judge those outside the church? *Are you not to judge those inside?* God will judge those outside. *"Expel the wicked man from among you."*

MATTHEW 18:15-18  If your *brother sins* against you, go and *show him his fault, just between the two of you.* If he listens to you, you have won your brother over.  But *if he will not listen, take one or two others along,* so that every matter may be established by the testimony of two or three *witnesses. If he refuses to listen to them, tell it to the church;* and *if he refuses to listen even to the church, treat him as you would a pagan or a tax collector.* I tell you the truth, *whatever you bind on earth will be bound in heaven,* and *whatever you loose on earth will be loosed in heaven.*

2 CORINTHIANS 2:6-8,10  The punishment inflicted on him by the majority is sufficient for him. Now instead, you ought to *forgive and comfort him,* so that he will not be overwhelmed by excessive sorrow. I urge you, therefore, to *reaffirm your love for him.* If you forgive anyone, I also forgive him.

God loves people and in that love commands church discipline and excommunication where needed. One who has committed a grievous sin or one who is not sorry for his sin should first be approached privately. If there is no success, two or three Christians should visit him. If he is still impenitent the church should speak to him. If the person still refuses to listen, the church is to remove (excommunicate) him from its fellowship. This action is as valid as if Christ Himself dealt with the person. If the excluded individual later confesses his sins and wants forgiveness, the congregation should assure him of God's love and theirs, and he should graciously be received back into the congregation.

## 6.  How does the local congregation publicly use these Keys?

1 CORINTHIANS 4:1  So then, men ought to *regard us as servants of Christ* and as those *entrusted with the secret things of God.*

ACTS 20:28 *Keep watch over yourselves* and *all the flock* of which the *Holy Spirit has made you overseers.* Be *shepherds* of the church of God.

EPHESIANS 4:11-12 It was *the Lord* who gave some to be *apostles,* some to be *prophets,* some to be *evangelists,* and some to be *pastors* and *teachers,* to *prepare God's people for works of service,* so that the *Body of Christ may be built up.*

Jesus authorized and commanded all believers individually and collectively to tell the Good News, to use the Sacraments, and to forgive or not forgive sin. The public use of these Keys is normally given to pastors. The Holy Spirit calls these men (divine call) to be pastors. They serve the Good Shepherd and are like shepherds for members of His flock. The holy ministry is the only office instituted by Christ. A congregation may, however, ask others to assist their pastor as Sunday School teachers, church officers, youth leaders, etc.

### Let's pray together

Dear Jesus, how great and wonderful and clean is Your Church. And to think that You have made us holy priests in it to serve You daily is a honor we do not deserve. You have also given us Keys which can lock and unlock the door to heaven by sharing the Good News, by baptizing and celebrating the Lord's Supper, and by forgiving and not forgiving sin. Help us use these Keys faithfully and wisely. Give us true compassion for the unconverted. When they come to faith may we joyfully assure them of their redemption and adoption. When it is necessary to exclude the impenitent from our fellowship, may we do so in love. Bless our pastor as the shepherd of this flock. Lord, join our hands with his hands that we may do all in our power to bring You to the lost and the lost to You. May we remain steadfast in the one true, saving faith to the end and finally wear the crown. For Your sake we ask it, Lord. Amen.

## Let's sing together

The Church's one foundation Is Jesus Christ her Lord;
She is His new creation By water and the Word.
From heav'n He came and sought her To be His holy bride;
With His own blood He bought her, And for her life He died.

Elect from ev'ry nation, Yet one o'er all the earth;
Her charter of salvation: One Lord, one faith, one birth.
One holy name she blesses, Partakes one holy food,
And to one hope she presses With ev'ry grace endued.

Yet she on earth has union With God, the Three in One,
And mystic sweet communion With those whose rest is won.
O blessed heavn'ly chorus! Lord, save us by Your grace
That we, like saints before us, May see You face to face.

## Bible reading schedule for the next seven days

- ❑ 1$^{st}$ day – Acts 10
- ❑ 2$^{nd}$ day – Acts 11
- ❑ 3$^{rd}$ day – Acts 12
- ❑ 4$^{th}$ day – Acts 13
- ❑ 5$^{th}$ day – Acts 14
- ❑ 6$^{th}$ day – Acts 15
- ❑ 7$^{th}$ day – Acts 16

## Worksheet no. 8

1. Every believer is a member of ( ) a Christian congregation, ( ) a Lutheran congregation, ( ) the invisible Church of Christ.

2. We become members of the one true invisible Church by ( ) Baptism, ( ) joining a Lutheran Church, ( ) going to church, ( ) faith in the Lord Jesus.

3. The Keys Jesus has given us give us the authority and power to do three things. They are:

   a. _____

   b. _____

c. _____

4. True or False: Christians can forgive sins in the name of Jesus.

5. What happens to the doors of heaven when sinners do not repent and believe? _____

6. True or False: The Keys which lock and unlock the doors to heaven have been placed in my hands.

7. List the three steps to be followed in carrying out church discipline:

a. _____

b. _____

c. _____

8. In one of the Bible verses we learned that _____ confessed his sin in the presence of _____ , and _____ assured _____ that God had forgiven him his sins.

9. The purposes of excommunication are to (   ) have the impenitent sinner see how great his sins are, (   ) keep him from going to church, (   ) keep him out of heaven, (   ) bring the person to repentance.

10. The sins of some church members today have been described as sins of commission, sins of omission, and sins of no mission.

What is meant by the last sin? _____

_____

11. Recently someone characterized many a modern congregation's view of their mission as that of assisting in "hatching, matching, and dispatching." What did he mean?

_____

_____

12. True or False: A congregation which does not go all out to evangelize its community with a dynamic witnessing program is forfeiting one of the basic reasons for its existence.

13. What is the main mission of the Church? _____

_____

14. What is a disciple? _____

_____

_____

15. True or False: The office of the holy ministry is a divine office.

16. A person says to you, "I think the important thing is that a minister be sincere. If he is sincere, any preacher can be my minister!" How would you respond? _____

_____

_____

*Lesson 9*

## I HAVE GOOD NEWS FOR YOU

# About A Stewardship Which Is Fully Committed

### 1. What is a Christian steward?

PSALM 24:1  The *earth is the LORD's, and everything in it,* the world, and *all who live in it.*

HAGGAI 2:8  "The *silver is Mine* and the *gold is Mine*" declares the LORD Almighty.

1 CHRONICLES 29:14  *Everything* comes *from You,* and *we have given You only what comes from Your hand.*

LUKE 12:48  From everyone who has been *given much, much will be demanded;* and from the one who has been entrusted with *much, much more* will be asked.

1 CORINTHIANS 10:31  Whether you eat or drink or *whatever you do, do it all for the glory of God.*

1 CORINTHIANS 4:2   It is required that those who have been *given a trust must prove faithful.*

●  2 CORINTHIANS 5:15  Christ died for all, that *those who live should no longer live for themselves* but *for Him* who died for them and was raised again.

JOHN 15:5,8  I am the vine; you are the branches. *If a man remains in Me and I in him, he will bear much fruit;* apart from Me you can do nothing. *This is to My Father's glory,* that you *bear much fruit, showing yourselves to be My disciples.*

ROMANS 14:12  So then, each of us will *give an account of himself* to God.

A steward is someone who takes care of another person's property and manages it the way the owner wants it managed. We are stewards for God here on earth. Everything belongs to God, and we do everything we can in our stewardship to honor Him. The secret to doing that is to live in and for Jesus. Then we will be ready for the Last Day when we give an account to the Lord.

## 2. What does God say about our use of time and abilities?

MATTHEW 25:14-15  Again, it will be like a man going on a journey, who called his servants and *entrusted his property* to them. To one he gave five talents of money ($10,000), to another two talents ($4,000), and to another one talent ($2,000), *each according to his ability.* Then he went on his journey.

1 CORINTHIANS 12:27,29-31 *You are the body of Christ,* and each one

of you is a part of it. Are all apostles? Are all prophets? Are all teachers? Do all work miracles? Do all have gifts of healing? Do all speak in tongues? Do all interpret? But *eagerly desire the greater gifts.*

1 PETER 4:10-11 Each one should *use whatever gift he has received to serve others, faithfully administering God's grace* in its various forms. If anyone speaks, he should do it as one speaking the very words of God. If anyone serves, he should do it with the strength God provides, *so that in all things God may be praised* through Jesus Christ.

EPHESIANS 5:15-17 *Be very careful, then, how you live* — not as unwise but as wise, *making the most of every opportunity*, because the days are evil. Therefore *do not be foolish*, but *understand what the Lord's will is.*

God gives all believers various gifts and abilities. He wants His lost sheep to be found and His Church to grow as His children use their gifts. His directive to you is to *discover and develop your more important gifts.* Don't waste time! Don't waste your gifts! God has a plan for you to serve. Spend more time discussing this with a mature Christian friend or your pastor.

### 3. What does God say about our serving Him with money?

If a Man's faith does not affect his pocketbook, then his faith is phony. ELTON TRUEBLOD

MARK 12:41 Jesus sat down opposite the place where the offerings were put and *watched the crowd putting their money into the temple treasury.*

PROVERBS 3:9 *Honor* the LORD with *your wealth*, with the *firstfruits* of all your crops.

MALACHI 3:8-10 "Will a man rob God? Yet you rob Me. But you ask, 'How do we rob You?' In *tithes and offerings.* You are under a curse — the whole nation of you — because you are robbing Me. Bring the *whole tithe* into the storehouse, that there may be food in My house. *Test Me in this*," says the LORD Almighty, "and see if I will not *throw open the floodgates of heaven* and pour out *so much blessing that you will not have room enough* for it."

LUKE 6:38  *Give,* and *it will be given to you.* A *good measure, pressed down, shaken together* and *running over,* will be *poured* into your lap. For with *the measure you use,* it will *be measured to you.*

1 CORINTHIANS 16:2  On the *first day* of *every week, each one* of you should *set aside* a sum of money *in keeping with his income.*

2 CORINTHIANS 9:7  *Each man should give* what he has *decided in his heart* to give, *not reluctantly* or *under compulsion,* for God *loves a cheerful giver.*

We honor God by giving our best gifts to Him. In the Old Testament this was the tithe (10%). Today we are free from the law to tithe, yet, many Christians still tithe and give more than the tithe because of their love for the Lord. A definite percent of one's income should be set aside for church work and charity. God says that Sunday is the day to bring these gifts to Him. He challenges us to give cheerfully, liberally, and to tithe, promising to give us more than we give Him.

## 4. What is our job as Christian witnesses?

MATTHEW 28:19-20  Jesus said, "Therefore *go* and *make disciples* of *all nations, baptizing* them in the name of the Father and of the Son and of the Holy Spirit, and *teaching* them to obey everything I have commanded you."

ACTS 1:8  You will receive *power* when the *Holy Spirit* comes on you; and *you will be My witnesses* in Jerusalem, and in all Judea and Samaria, and to the ends of the earth.

LUKE 5:10-11  Jesus said to Simon, "Don't be afraid; from now on you will catch men." So they pulled their boats up on shore, *left everything* and *followed Him.*

MATTHEW 9:36-38  When *Jesus saw the crowds, He had compassion* on them, because they were harassed and helpless, like sheep without a shepherd. Then He said to His disciples, "The *harvest is plentiful* but the *workers are few. Ask* the Lord of the harvest, therefore, to *send out workers* into His harvest field."

JOHN 4:35  Do you not say, "Four months more and then the harvest"? I tell you, *open your eyes* and *look at the fields!* They are *ripe for harvest.*

ROMANS 1:14-15  I am *obligated* both to *Greeks* and *non-Greeks,* both to the *wise* and the *foolish.* That is why I am so *eager to preach the Gospel* also to you who are at Rome.

ROMANS 10:1  Brothers, my *heart's desire* and *prayer* to God for the Israelites is that *they may be saved.*

What was the definition of a disciple from the previous Lesson? With that definition in mind, know that it is God's divine will to win the world to Himself. It is God's desire to have the Gospel of Christ come to you and then go through you and on to many others. The Lord wants you to be a fisher of men, not just a "keeper of an aquarium." All who follow Jesus take these words seriously. This is not a game. Evangelism is to be the prime work of every Christian and every Christian congregation.

## 5. What should we do as Christian witnesses?

ACTS 10:39  We are *witnesses* of everything He did in the country of the Jews and in Jerusalem.

ACTS 4:20  For we *cannot help speaking* about what *we have seen* and *heard.*

JOHN 4:28-29,39  The woman went back to the town and said to the people, "*Come, see* a Man who *told me everything I ever did.*"... *Many* of the Samaritans from that town *believed* in Jesus *because of the woman's testimony,* "He told me everything I ever did."

2 CORINTHIANS 5:19-20  God has *committed to us* the message of reconciliation. We are therefore *Christ's ambassadors,* as though God were *making His appeal through us.*

1 CORINTHIANS 9:19-20,22  Though I am free and belong to no man, I *make myself a slave to everyone,* to *win as many as possible.* To the Jews I became like a Jew, to win the Jews... To the weak I became weak, to win the weak. I have become *all things* to *all men* so that by *all possible means* I might *save some.*

COLOSSIANS 4:5  *Be wise* in the way you *act* toward outsiders; *make the most of every opportunity.*

A Christian witness knows Jesus and shares that knowledge with other people. An ambassador for Christ is His envoy, represents Him, and speaks for Him. I am His witness and ambassador by virtue of my faith in the Lord. I have a story to tell, and there are people waiting for me to tell it. My goal should be to speak to people about Jesus at every opportunity. I will also invite people to my church. Over 70% of the people who join a church came the first time as a result of a simple invitation by one of its members.

## 6. Why do we want to be good Christian stewards?

MATTHEW 25:19-21  After a long time the master of those servants *returned and settled accounts* with them. The man who had received the five talents brought the other five. "Master," he said, "you entrusted me with five talents. *See, I have gained five more.*" His master replied, "*Well done, good and faithful servant!* You have been faithful with a few things; I will *put you in charge of many things. Come and share your master's happiness!*"

LUKE 18:28-30  Peter said to Him, "We have left all we had to follow You!" "I tell you the truth," Jesus said to them, "No one who has left home or wife or brothers or parents or children for the sake of the Kingdom of God will fail *to receive many times as much in this age* and, in the age to come, *eternal life.*"

DANIEL 12:3  Those who *lead many to righteousness* will *shine like the stars for ever and ever.*

GALATIANS 6:9  Let us not become weary in doing good, for at the proper time we *will reap a harvest* if we *do not give up.*

● 1 CORINTHIANS 15:58  Therefore, my dear brothers, *stand firm.* Let *nothing move you.* Always *give yourselves fully* to the work of the Lord, because you know that *your labor in the Lord is not in vain.*

> J - esus
> O - thers
> Y - ourself

Some day the Lord will return for an accounting. Faithful stewards will hear Jesus commend and praise them. He promises to give countless rewards to faithful stewards already in this life. Faithful stewards should feel encouraged and never give up their work for Jesus. Faithful stewards also lay up rewards in heaven. What a kind and gracious God we have. No work for Him is ever wasted.

## Let's pray together

Heavenly Father, thank You for teaching me what it means to be a good Christian steward. I believe You own everything. I want to honor You by the way I live and the way I give. Every ability I have is a gift from You. I commit myself and my skills to You in daily service. I want to dedicate a large percent of my income to You as an expression of my love. Help me be a good witness for Jesus. Bless my efforts to bring people to trust in Him. When I feel discouraged, please encourage me and graciously bless my work. Thank You, God, for everything! I pray in Jesus' name. Amen.

## Let's sing together

Lord of the living harvest That whitens on the plain,
Where angels soon shall gather Their sheaves of golden grain,
Accept our hands to labor, Our hearts to trust and love,
And with us ever hasten Your Kingdom from above.

As lab'rers in Your vineyard, Help us be ever true,
Content to bear the burden Of weary days for You.
To ask no other wages When You will call us home
Than to have shared the labor That makes Your Kingdom come.

Be with us, God the Father, Be with us, God the Son,
And God the Holy Spirit, Most blessed Three in One.
Teach us, as faithful servants You rightly to adore,
And fill us with Your fullness Both now and evermore.

## Bible reading schedule for the next seven days

❏  1st day – Acts 17          ❏  5th day – Acts 21
❏  2nd day – Acts 18          ❏  6th day – Acts 22
❏  3rd day – Acts 19          ❏  7th day – Acts 23
❏  4th day – Acts 20

## Worksheet no. 9

1. Since God is the Owner of everything, what rule should we follow in using anything in this world? _____

2. Name some special gifts and abilities that you may have to serve the Lord as a good steward: _____

3. True or False: Christian stewardship is dedicating everything we have to God's glory, the building of His Kingdom, our neighbor's welfare and our own good welfare out of love for Jesus Christ.

4. As Jesus watches you give your offerings in His Father's House, how do think He feels? What changes, if any, do you feel are necessary on your part? _____

5. What are some of the chief thieves which sometimes needlessly rob us of time? _____

6. True or False: I really believe the Lord wants me to speak to others about Him as best I can and that He will give me the strength to do so.

7. True or False: We should share Christ with all people, even those who have membership in another church.

8. What is the greatest gift we can give a person? _____

9. What can we do to become more efficient in our witnessing for Christ? _____

10. Should it bother us to know when certain people are living without the Lord Jesus? _____ Why? _____

11. As you speak to a friend about believing in Jesus he says, "I have plenty of time. I'll take my chances." What would you say to him? _____

    _____

12. What is meant by spontaneous witnessing? _____

13. What truths should we stress when speaking to folks about Jesus? _____

    _____

14. How do you suppose you will feel in heaven if someone is there because God used your voice to speak to him about Christ? ____

    _____

    _____

15. Mention three things that you will surely want to do before leaving this life for heaven:

    a. _____

b. _____

c. _____

*Lesson 10*

## I HAVE GOOD NEWS FOR YOU

# About A Life Which Never Ends

### 1. What happens at the moment of death?

ECCLESIASTES 12:7  The *dust* returns to the *ground* it came from, and the *spirit returns to God* who gave it.

2 CORINTHIANS 5:8  We are *confident,* I say, and would *prefer to be away from the body* and at *home with the Lord.*

PSALM 23:4-6 Even though I walk through the valley of the shadow of death, *I will fear no evil, for You are with me; Your rod and Your staff, they comfort me...* and *I will dwell in the house of the LORD forever.*

● LUKE 23:43 Jesus answered him, "I tell you the truth, *today* you will be *with Me in paradise*."

REVELATION 14:13 Then I heard a voice from heaven say, "Write: *Blessed* are the dead who *die in the Lord* from now on." "Yes," says the Spirit, "they will *rest from their labor*, for their *deeds will follow them*."

1 PETER 3:19 He (Jesus) went and preached to the *spirits in prison*.

At the moment of death the body begins to return to dust. The believer is at once received into heaven, and the unbeliever is at once imprisoned in hell.

### What they said at death's door

THOMAS PAINE, American infidel and author: "I would give worlds, if I had them that 'The Age of Reason' had never been published. O God, what have I done to suffer so much? But there is no God! But if there should be, what will become of me hereafter? Stay with me, for God's sake! Send even a child to stay with me, for it is Hell to be alone. If ever the Devil had an agent, I have been that one."

FRANCIS VOLTAIRE, noted French infidel and writer said to his doctor: "I am abandoned by God and man! I will give you half of what I am worth if you will give me six months' life. Then I shall go to Hell; and you will go with me. O Christ! O Jesus Christ!"

DWIGHT L. MOODY, great preacher: "I see earth receding. Heaven is opening. God is calling!"

Adroniram Judson, great American missionary to Burma: "I go with the gladness of a boy bounding away from school. I feel so strong in Christ."

### 2. What does the Bible say about Christ's second coming?

ACTS 1:11 "Men of Galilee," they said, "why do you stand here

looking into the sky? This same Jesus, who has been taken from you into heaven, *will come back in the same way* you have seen Him go into heaven."

REVELATION 1:7 Look, He is coming with the clouds, and *every eye will see Him*, even those who pierced Him.

ACTS 17:31 For *God has set a day* when *He will judge the world* with *justice* by the *Man* He has appointed.

MARK 13:32-33 *No one knows* about that day or hour, not even the angels in heaven, nor the Son, but only the Father. *Be on guard! Be alert! You do not know* when that time will come.

2 PETER 3:10-11 The day of the Lord will come like a *thief*. The *heavens* will *disappear* with a roar; the *elements* will be *destroyed* by fire, and the *earth* and *everything in it* will be *laid bare*. Since *everything will be destroyed* in this way, what kind of people ought you to be? You ought to *live holy* and *godly lives*.

1 PETER 4:7 The *end* of all things is *near*.

Jesus will come again in great glory. Everyone will see Him. He will judge all men. The date, known only to God, will come suddenly and unexpectedly, and will bring an end to the world and the universe. We are encouraged to lead a godly life and stand in readiness.

## 3. What about the resurrection of the body?

JOHN 5:28-29 A time is coming when *all who are in their graves* will *hear His voice and come out* — those who have done good will *rise to live,* and those who have done evil will *rise to be condemned.*

JOB 19:25-27 I know that *my Redeemer lives,* and that in the end He will stand upon the earth. And after my skin has been destroyed, yet *in my flesh I will see God;* I myself will see Him *with my own eyes* —

I, and not another. How my heart yearns within me!

PHILIPPIANS 3:20-21  Our *citizenship* is in heaven. And we eagerly await a Savior from there, the Lord Jesus Christ, who... will *transform our lowly bodies* so that they will *be like His glorious body.*

1 CORINTHIANS 15:51-52  Listen, I tell you a mystery: We will not all sleep, but we will *all be changed* — in a *flash*, in the *twinkling of an eye*, at the last trumpet. For the trumpet will sound, the dead will be *raised imperishable*, and we *will be changed.*

On the Last Day all the dead will hear Jesus. They will be told to come out of their graves to be reunited with their souls. The bodies of the believers will change, have no more sin, sickness, or death. The same change will occur to the bodies of believers living on earth on this Day.

## 4.  What will happen on Judgment Day?

2 CORINTHIANS 5:10  For *we must all appear* before the judgment seat of Christ.

ACTS 17:31  For God has *set a day* when He will *judge the world* with *justice* by the *Man* He has appointed.

JOHN 12:48  There is a *judge* for the one who rejects Me and does not accept My words; that *very word* which I spoke *will condemn him* at the last day.

MARK 16:16  Whoever *believes* and is baptized *will be saved*, but whoever *does not believe will be condemned.*

MATTHEW 25:31-34,41  When the Son of Man comes in His glory, and all the angels with Him, He will sit on His throne in heavenly glory. *All the nations* will be *gathered before Him*, and He will *separate the people* one from another as a shepherd *separates the sheep from the goats.* He will put the *sheep on His right* and the *goats on His left.*

Then the King will say to those on His right, "*Come, you who are blessed by My Father; take your inheritance, the Kingdom prepared for you since the creation of the world.*"... Then He will say to those on His left, "*Depart from Me, you who are cursed,* into the *eternal fire prepared for the devil and his angels.*"

LUKE 16:22-24  The beggar *died* and the *angels carried him* to *Abraham's side.* The rich man also *died* and was buried. In *hell,* where *he was in torment,* he looked up and saw Abraham far away, with Lazarus by his side. So he called to him, "Father Abraham, *have pity on me* and send Lazarus to dip the tip of his finger in water and cool my tongue, because *I am in agony in this fire.*"

MATTHEW 10:28  Do not be afraid of those who kill the body but cannot kill the soul. Rather, be afraid of the One who can *destroy both soul and body in hell.*

ISAIAH 66:24  Their worm (guilty conscience) *will not die, nor will their fire be quenched,* and they will be *loathsome to all* mankind.

MATTHEW 7:13-14  Enter through the *narrow gate.* For *wide is the gate* and *broad is the road* that *leads to destruction,* and *many enter through it.* But *small is the gate* and *narrow the road* that *leads to life,* and *only a few find it.*

Everyone, all believers and all unbelievers, will stand before Christ for judgment. Jesus will look for saving faith and the fruits of saving faith. There are today and will be then only two camps: saved or unsaved, fruits of faith or lack of them, sheep or goats, blessed or cursed, the glory of heaven or the torment of hell.

## 5. What will heaven be like?

JOHN 14:2  In My Father's *house are many rooms;* if it were not so, I would have told you. *I am going there to prepare a place for you.*

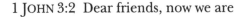

1 JOHN 3:2  Dear friends, now we are

children of God, and *what we will be has not yet been made known.* But we know that when He appears, *we shall be like Him,* for *we shall see Him* as He is.

ALLELUIA

REVELATION 7:9-10  Before me was a *great multitude* that no one could count, from every nation, tribe, people and language, standing before the throne and in front of the Lamb. They were wearing *white robes* and were holding *palm branches* in their hands. And *they cried out in a loud voice: "Salvation belongs to our God,* who sits on the throne, and *to the Lamb."*

REVELATION 7:16-17  *Never again will they hunger,* never again will they *thirst.* The sun will not beat upon them, nor any scorching heat. For the Lamb at the center of the throne will be their *Shepherd; He will lead them to springs of living water.* And *God will wipe away every tear from their eyes.*

REVELATION 21:3-5  And I heard a loud voice from the throne saying, "Now the *dwelling of God is with men,* and *He will live with them. They will be His people,* and God Himself will be with them and be their God. He will *wipe every tear from their eyes.* There will be *no more death or mourning or crying or pain, for the old order of things has passed away."* He who was seated on the throne said, "*I am making everything new!"* Then He said, "Write this down, for *these words are trustworthy and true."*  (For a more complete description read all of Chapter 21.)

PSALM 16:11  You have made known to me the path of life; You will *fill me with joy in Your presence,* with *eternal pleasures at Your right hand.*

PSALM 17:15  In *righteousness I will see Your face,* when I awake, *I will be satisfied with seeing Your likeness.*

ROMANS 8:18  I consider that our present sufferings are not worth comparing with *the glory that will be revealed in us.*

Heaven is God's home, a place of entrancing beauty. It will be filled with a huge crowd of people who came from all over the earth because salvation came to them, and now they offer perfect praise to God and the Lamb who made it all possible. We will be totally satisfied and happy and will live intimately with God. Our greatest joy in heaven will be the joy God's presence brings us. We shall live in indescribable joy and glory. Or...

**THINK**
Of stepping on a shore and finding it heaven;
Of taking hold of a hand and finding it God's hand;
Of breathing a new air and finding it celestial air;
Of feeling invigorated and finding it immortality;
Of passing from storm and tempest to an unbroken calm;
Of waking up and finding it Home!

### 6. To whom will God give eternal life?

JOHN 3:16  For God so loved the world that He gave His one and only Son, that *whoever believes in Him* shall not perish but have *eternal life.*

JOHN 3:36  Whoever *believes in the Son has eternal life,* but whoever *rejects the Son will not see life,* for *God's wrath remains* on him.

God gives eternal life only to those who believe on His Son, Jesus Christ, as their personal Lord and Savior.

### 7. What, then, should be some important goals in our lives?

● ACTS 16:31  *Believe in the Lord Jesus,* and you will be saved.

REVELATION 2:10  *Be faithful, even to the point of death,* and I will give you the crown of life.

MARK 16:15-16  *Go into all the world and preach the Good News* to all creation. *Whoever believes and is baptized will be saved,* but *whoever does not believe will be condemned.*

REVELATION 22:20-21  He who testifies to these things says, "Yes, *I am coming soon.*" Amen. *Come, Lord Jesus.* The grace of the Lord Jesus be with God's people. Amen.

We should make absolutely sure that we believe on the Lord Jesus for salvation and that we remain faithful to Him to the end. We should do everything we can to personally win the lost for their Savior and heaven. All who believe in Him and are baptized will be saved. We should joyfully look forward to the time when Jesus comes to take us to our eternal Home. May each of us in this class pass through those pearly gates to live forever with our Lord, live with each other, and with all those we brought to Jesus.

## Let's pray together

Lord Jesus, our precious Savior, we thank You with all our might for this Bible study course and in particular for this last Lesson. Thank You for warning us about the anguish of Hell. Thank You for telling us about the glory of Heaven. What a beautiful city Jerusalem must be. Thank You for describing what we will be like and for the description of the activity which takes place there continually. Please strengthen our faith in You in the days ahead through good Bible study. Please give us power to live for You. Please use each of us to tell others about You so that they may be saved, too. Finally, Lord, when life is over, take each of us to our beautiful home in Heaven where we will eternally thank and praise You, the Father, and the Holy Spirit. Hear us, Lord Jesus! Amen! Amen! Amen!

## Let's sing together

Abide with me, fast falls the eventide. The darkness deepens; Lord with me abide. When other helpers fail and comforts flee, Help of the helpless, oh, abide with me.

Swift to its close ebbs out life's little day; Earth's joys grow dim,
Its glories pass away. Change and decay in all around I see;
O Thou who changest not, abide with me.

I fear no foe with Thee at hand to bless; Ills have no weight, And
tears no bitterness. Where is death's sting? Where grave thy
victory? I triumph still if Thou abide with me.

Hold Thou Thy cross before my closing eyes; Shine through the
gloom, And point me to the skies; Heav'n's morning breaks, and
earth's vain shadows flee; In life, in death, O Lord, abide with me.

## Bible reading for the next few days

Revelation 19, 20, 21, 22, and Psalm 23

## Worksheet no. 10

1. When we die _____ and _____ separate. Our _____

   goes to heaven, and our _____ returns to dust.

2. True or False: Unbelievers are given another chance to be
   saved after they die.

3. A person says, "I don't really care if I go to heaven or not."

   How would you reply? _____

   _____

4. True or False: Unbelievers will be condemned to everlasting
   death by Christ on Judgment Day for not believing in Him as
   their Savior and for not living their lives to His glory.

5. Read 1 Corinthians 15:56-57. Where does death get its power?

   _____ Where do we Christians get our victory? _____

6. When Scripture speaks of hell as everlasting fire and
   punishment with intense pain and weeping (     ) it is an effort

on God's part to make men fear ever going to such a place, ( ) it is an overstatement of truth, ( ) it is an effort to describe the true and terrible conditions of all those who die without Christ.

7. What passages from this Lesson prove that when Christ returns He will not reign on this earth for a thousand years (millennium) as some people believe He will? _____

_____

8. What are some of the joys we will experience in heaven? ____

_____

_____

_____

9. True or False: Because Christ rose from the dead, all Christians are positively assured of their redemption, resurrection, and new life in heaven.

10. Read Daniel 12:3b. What, hopefully, will be one of your greatest joys in heaven? _____

_____

11. Survey your friends, acquaintances, people you know. Jot down the first names of just three of them who may not know Jesus personally as their Savior: _____

Mention at least two things you can do to help them find Jesus:

a. _____

b. _____

12. If you knew you would die at the end of this year, how would your life change (try to mention specifics)? _____

_____

_____

13. If you were granted just one wish, what would the wish be?

    _____

    How could this wish become reality? _____

    _____

14. In view of everything learned in this Bible study, mention at least four important goals for your life that you want to pursue from here on:

    a. _____

    b. _____

    c. _____

    d. _____

# Apostles' Creed

### The First Article

CREATION AND PRESERVATION

**I believe in God, the Father Almighty, Maker of heaven and earth.**

*What does this mean?* I believe that God has made me and all creatures; that He has given me my body and soul, eyes, ears, and all my members, my reason and all my senses, and still takes care of them. He also gives me clothing and shoes, food and drink, house and home, wife and children, land, animals, and all that I have. He richly and daily provides me with all that I need to support this body and life. He defends me against all danger and guards and protects me from all evil. All this He does only out of fatherly, divine goodness and mercy, without any merit or worthiness in me. For all this it is my duty to thank and praise, serve and obey Him. This is most certainly true.

### The Second Article

REDEMPTION

**I believe in Jesus Christ, His only Son, our Lord, who was conceived by the Holy Spirit, born of the virgin Mary, suffered under Pontius Pilate, was crucified, died and was buried. He descended into hell. The third day He rose again from the dead. He ascended into heaven and sits at the right hand of God, the Father Almighty. From thence He will come to judge the**

**living and the dead.**

*What does this mean?* I believe that Jesus Christ, true God, begotten of the Father from eternity, and also true man, born of the virgin Mary, is my Lord, who has redeemed me, a lost and condemned person, purchased and won me from all sins, from death, and from the power of the devil; not with gold or silver, but with His holy, precious blood and with His innocent suffering and death, that I may be His own, and live under Him in His Kingdom, and serve Him in everlasting righteousness, innocence, and blessedness, just as He is risen from the dead, lives and reigns to all eternity. This is most certainly true.

## The Third Article

### SANCTIFICATION

**I believe in the Holy Spirit, the holy Christian Church, the communion of saints, the forgiveness of sins, the resurrection of the body, and the life everlasting. Amen.**

*What does this mean?* I believe that I cannot by my own reason or strength believe in Jesus Christ, my Lord, or come to Him; but the Holy Spirit has called me by the Gospel, enlightened me with His gifts, sanctified and kept me in the true faith. In the same way He calls, gathers, enlightens, and sanctifies the whole Christian Church on earth, and keeps it with Jesus Christ in the one true faith. In this Christian Church He daily and riches forgives all my sins and the sins of all believers. On the Last Day He will raise me and all the dead, and give eternal life to me and all believers in Christ. This is most certainly true.

# Nicene Creed

I believe in one God, the Father Almighty, maker of heaven and earth and of all things visible and invisible.

And in one Lord Jesus Christ, the only-begotten Son of God, begotten of His Father before all worlds, God of God, Light of Light, very God of very God, begotten, not made, being of one substance with the Father, by whom all things were made; who for us men and for our salvation came down from heaven and was incarnate by the Holy Spirit of the virgin Mary and was made man; and was crucified also for us under Pontius Pilate. He suffered and was buried. And the third day He rose again according to the Scriptures and ascended into heaven and sits at the right hand of the Father. And He will come again with glory to judge both the living and the dead, whose Kingdom will have no end.

And I believe in the Holy Spirit, the Lord and giver of life, who proceeds from the Father and the Son, who with the Father and Son together is worshiped and glorified, who spoke by the prophets. And I believe in one holy Christian and apostolic Church, I acknowledge one Baptism for the remission of sins, and I look for the resurrection of the dead and the life of the world to come. Amen.

# Bible Readings For Assistance In Life

## What to read when —

**The future seems hopeless**
1 Peter 1:3-9; 5:10,11; Isaiah 54:1-7; Lamentations 3:19-24

**Seeking God's direction**
Romans 12:1-3; Ephesians 5:15-17; Proverbs 2:1-6

**You are in danger**
Luke 8:22-25; Psalm 91

**You need comfort**
2 Corinthians 1:3-7; 7:6-13; Isaiah 12; 40:1-11

**Others disagree with you**
Matthew 7:1-5; Romans 12:9-21; 14:1-15:7

**The world seems enticing**
2 Corinthians 6:14-7:1; James 4:4-10; 1 John 2:15-17

**You need assurance of salvation**
John 3:14-21; 11:25,26; 1John 5:9-13; Psalm 91:14-16

**Others have sinned against you**
Matthew 6:14,15; 18:21-35; Colossians 3:12-14

**You are tempted to be bitter**
1 Corinthians 13; Ephesians 4:29-5:2

**You are tempted to neglect public worship**
Acts 2:42-47; Hebrews 10:19-25; Psalm 95:1-7

**You need to control your tongue**

Matthew 15:1-20; James 3:1-12

**Your faith needs to be strengthened**
Romans 5:1-11; 1 Corinthians 9:24-27; Hebrews 10:19-25,35-39; 11:1-12:13

**You are prone to judge others**
Matthew 7:1-5; 1 Corinthians 4:1-5; James 2:1-13; 4:11,12

**You have been cheated**
1 Corinthians 6:1-8; James 5:1-8

**Things are going well**
Luke 12:13-21; 1 Timothy 6:3-19; James 2:1-17

**You wonder about your spiritual gifts**
Romans 12:3-8; 1 Corinthians 12:1-14:25; 1 Peter 4:7-11

**Starting a new job**
Matthew 5:13-16; Galatians 5:13-26; 1 Kings 3:1-14

**You have a position of responsibility**
Mark 10:35-45; 1 Corinthians 16:13,14; Galatians 6:9,10; Proverbs 3:21-27

**You are married**
Ephesians 5:22-6:4; 1 Peter 3:1-7; Ecclesiastes 9:7-10

**You have been quarreling**
Ephesians 4:1-6, 4:15-5:2; 2 Timothy 2:14-26; James 4:1-12

**You are challenged by evil**
Romans 8:38,39; 2 Corinthians 4:7-18; Ephesians 6:10-18

**You are jealous**
Galatians 5:13-15, 19-21; James 3:13-18

**You struggle with laziness**
1 Thessalonians 4:1-12; 2 Thessalonians 3:6-15

**You struggle with lust**
    Matthew 5:27-30; Romans 7:7-25; 13:8-14; James 1:13-18

**You are angry**
    Matthew 18:21-35; Genesis 4:1-12

**A loved one in Christ has died**
    John 11:1-44; Revelation 19:1-9, 21, 21

**Preparing for the Lord' Supper**
    1 Corinthians 11:23-32; Matthew 26:17-30

This Bible study written by Pastor Ginkel
120 pages, Leader's Guide available

# The Story of Angels

Because of the intense interest in this topic, most study groups using this book double and even triple in size. Colorful and descriptive flyers permit you to imprint time and location of your class on your copy machine and may be used as handouts and bulletin inserts.

•◆ **THEIR BEGINNING AND BEING**
Their creation, their purpose, their home, their properties

•◆ **SATAN AND THE FALLEN ANGELS**
Their fall, their names, their power, their knowledge, on the attack, their defeat

•◆ **ANGEL TITLES, NAMES, AND ACTIVITIES**
Who they are, Michael, Gabriel, Cherubim, Seraphim

•◆ **THE ANGEL OF THE LORD**
Who He is and what He did in the Old Testament

•◆ **GUARDING AND AVENGING ANGELS**
Old and New Testament examples of what they did

•◆ **WATCHING AND COMMUNICATING ANGELS**
Old and New Testament examples of what they did

•◆ **ANGELS AND JESUS**
Before His birth, at His birth, lower than the angels, the temptation, in Gethsemane, at His resurrection and His ascension

•◆ **EVIL ANGELS TODAY**
Warning, the occult, witchcraft, Mormonism, New Age, Demon possession, near death experiences, Satan and Satanism, our victory

•◆ **ANGELS AND BELIEVERS TODAY**
Rejoicing, watching, guarding, and delivering

•◆ **ON JUDGMENT DAY AND FOREVER**
Introducing the Day, divide believers from unbelievers, execute judgment, evil angels, holy angels, our privilege and honor, closing thoughts

This Bible study written by Pastor Ginkel
Part 1 80 pages & Part 2 80 pages, Leader's Guide available

# A Time To Laugh... Or Cry

What a delight it is to laugh and laugh hard. What a relief it is to cry and cry hard. *A Time To Laugh... or Cry* overviews the activity of man in the Old Testament — a time to cry because of man's stubbornness and sin and a time to laugh because of God's reaction to man's sin expressed in the Messiah. The thread of the Messiah is followed throughout. Each lesson begins with a contemporary introduction, hymn, prayer, explanation of text, probing and practical questions for discussion, plan of action, and daily Bible reading which correlates with the text being studied. A good dose of humor is interspersed throughout to attract attention and maintain interest.

**Part 1**  In the Beginning With Adam and Eve
In the Garden When Everything Went Wrong
At the Flood with Noah
When God Made A Promise to Abraham
When Abraham Faced the Supreme Test
When Jacob Received the Biggest Blessing
With Joseph the Slave, Prisoner, and Prime Minister
When God Called Moses to Lead Israel
When Israel Was Saved by the Blood of the Lamb
When God Gave the Law on Sinai

**Part 2**  When Israel Conquered Canaan
With Gideon, God's Man of Action
With Samson, Strong and Foolish
With David, the Soldier Boy and King
During the Building & Dedication of Solomon's Temple
At a Daring Contest of the Prophet Elijah
With Jonah, the Reluctant Evangelist
At What Isaiah Saw and Said
With Faithful Daniel and His Friends
At Malachi's Message of Despair and Hope

This Bible study written by Pastor Ginkel
112 pages, Leader's Guide available

# The Many Wonders of Heaven

ALLELUIA

Going to heaven is the greatest experience ever! Just the mention of the word boggles our minds and moves our hearts. What will we be? What will we have? What will we do? This study concentrates on the questions and answers, and it emphasizes the joy of your future home.

### ❖ THE WONDER OF ENTRANCE

Impossible Because of Sin, Now Possible Because of Jesus, Journey Begins At Conversion, Entrance Into Heaven Occurs At Death, Journey Complete At The Resurrection.

### ❖ THE WONDER OF GOD

Soon and Very Soon, His Glory, His Holiness, His Love, His Throne, His Dwelling Place, His Temple.

### ❖ THE WONDER OF THE SAINTS

I'd Rather Be..., Names Written, Citizenship, Bride of Christ, Permanent Dwelling Places, Their Condition — Perfect Joy, Pleasure, Complete Knowledge, New Bodies, New Heart, Christlike.

### ❖ THE WONDER OF GOD'S FAMILY

God, Angels, Animals, People — Numbers, Identity and Recognition, Happy Reunion, Unity, Marriage Temporary, Conversation, Laughter, Joy.

### ❖ THE WONDER OF REWARD

Introductory Thoughts, Service Here — Rewards There, Various Rewards, Served By Jesus, Motivation.

### ❖ THE WONDER OF ACTIVITY

Will It Really Be Rest, Fellowship, Eating, Rejoicing, Worship and Praise, Serving, Reigning.

### ❖ THE WONDER OF THE CITY

The Best Is Yet To Come, Prophesied, Revelation 21 — 22:6 Describes The City — Multiples of Twelve, The Temple, The River, The Fruit, Paradise Regained and More!

### ❖ THE WONDER OF ANTICIPATION

Be Watchful, Living Properly In The Last Days, Do Not Lose Heart, Sharing The Saving Gospel, Longing For A Better Country, The Assurance of Salvation, He Loves Me Always, The End is Near, What Will Happen.

This Bible study written by Pastor Ginkel
128 pages, Leader's Guide available

# Getting Closer To God

Contains the basic truths of Scripture for juniors and adults. Passages are printed out with summary thoughts, suggested passages for memorization, closing hymn, prayer, Bible reading schedule for the week, and challenging worksheet questions.

Course fosters a clear, concise understanding of basic Christian doctrine in catechetical form with a strong emphasis on forgiveness of sins through Jesus alone in every lesson. A dose of humor is used throughout without showing disrespect for the teachings of Scripture.

## GETTING CLOSER TO GOD

This Bible study written by Pastor James Knotek
166 pages

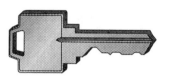

# Unlocking the Mystery of Revelation

Here is a Bible study which covers all of Revelation. Discussion questions at the end of each chapter. Excellent for Bible classes or individual study. Reflects a sound, Biblical method of interpretation allowing Scripture to interpret Scripture.

"I want to express my gratitude for *Unlocking the Mystery of Revelation.* I've been reading it and intend to use it as a source book for my fall Bible class. It's a **monumentum opus**! Congratulations on a beautiful job for Christ and His Church."

Dr. Oswald Waech

"Just a note to let you know how much I'm enjoy the study of Revelation by Pastor Knotek! Time flies so fast during the study that I can hardly wait for the next day!"

Dr. William Malcom, Jr.

"I want you to know how invaluable your book has been to our understanding of Revelation. I am one of the teaching leaders, and I personally was feeling somewhat overwhelmed last fall when I saw an ad for your book. Your material really helped things fall into place for me and for many in the class as well. Thank you!"

Marilyn Plechas

**To order these Bible studies and other Christian materials and a brochure call our toll free number: 1-888-772-8878**